4th Edition

Yardsticks

Child and Adolescent Development Ages 4–14

CHIP WOOD

Center for Responsive Schools, Inc.

All net proceeds from the sale of this book support the work of Center for Responsive Schools, Inc., a not-for-profit educational organization and the developer of the *Responsive Classroom* approach to teaching.

The stories in this book are all based on real events. However, to respect students' privacy, names and many identifying characteristics of students and situations have been changed.

ISBN: 978-1-892989-89-5
Library of Congress Control Number: 2017945943

Thanks to all the families who allowed us to use their children's artwork and photos within this book.

Center for Responsive Schools, Inc.
85 Avenue A, P.O. Box 718
Turners Falls, MA 01376-0718

800-360-6332
www.responsiveclassroom.org

Fifth printing 2021

For Lily, turning thirteen

✳

CONTENTS

✳

Preface to the Fourth Edition

Welcome! Here is a book approaching twenty-five years in print, now in its fourth edition. It has been read by over 350,000 people who care deeply about children. You're in good company. Whether you are a teacher or parent, school administrator or school volunteer, you will find much to think about as you read.

It's a privilege for me to have a few minutes to talk with you before you read on. While I want to provide you with a glimpse into the impetus for this book, my main objective is to challenge you to think about how you might share some of what you learn in these pages to advocate for the needs of your own children and/or the children and families in your school if you are a teacher, staff member, administrator, or school board member. Knowledge is power, but only if put to use collectively.

The genesis for this book grew out of such a collective experience and the commitment of a handful of teachers, who in 1981 co-founded a K–8 independent laboratory school in Greenfield, Massachusetts. The school was founded on the principles of child development that you will read about in this book. We believed then, as now, that understanding the relationship between children's growth and the approach to teaching and learning being used in classrooms can help educators and parents understand, create, and protect the kind of educational environments in which children can thrive.

A little over two hundred years ago, pioneers in philosophy, psychology, child development, and education in Europe and America began investigating the lives of children at home and in school. Through observing and recording children in these settings, making hypotheses, and drawing some conclusions about what they saw children do and heard them say, treatises emerged that spoke of children's inherent capacities and indomitable spirits. Darwin and Rousseau wrote about their own children in the 17th and 18th centuries. Montessori wrote about children in her schools in Italy and Piaget tried out his theories with his own and other children in France. Little is written about early research in child development in Africa, Asia, or South America, to our detriment, except through works by western anthropologists such as Margaret Mead and Barbara Rogoff.

Among the first pioneers in child development and education in America were two young educators, Beatrice Chandler Gesell and Arnold Gesell, who in 1912 authored *The Normal Child and Primary Education* based on their work at Los Angeles State Normal School (Teachers College) and their experience with John Dewey's school in Chicago. This amazing early work champions the child. They write, "The primary child has many untouched reservoirs of interest and capacity. He is ripe for unguessed avenues of activity and attainment" (Gesell and Gesell 1912). Such positivity is also reflected in Arnold Gesell's many books and work in child development at Yale University where, as a medical doctor and researcher, he created the first normative scales of physical, language, and behavioral development, still in use today.

Yardsticks draws from this body of work and equally from the influences of Lev Vygotsky, Maria Montessori, Erik Erikson, Lucy Sprague Mitchell, Caroline Pratt, and John Dewey, as well as from contemporaries such as James P. Comer, Rachael Kessler, Beverly Daniel Tatum, Sonia Nieto, and William Crain—all of whom champion the capacity of children to explore, discover, and be nurtured in active, engaging classrooms.

Education in the 20th and 21st centuries, of course, has been more heavily influenced by measures of intelligence and achievement than scales of development. In examining the origins of standardized testing in the 19th century, a 1992 U.S. government report states, "The American pursuit of efficiency . . . would create the world's most fertile ground for the cultivation of educational tests" (US Congress Office of Technology Assessment 1992).

Teachers' accountability for student achievement—measured at earlier and earlier grade levels by standardized assessments, both formative and summative, in all core subjects with attendant test-prep booklets, curriculum pacing charts, and recording requirements—is eroding quality teaching time and leaving teachers feeling disempowered and discouraged by their growing lack of autonomy in the classroom.

This illustration captures the strengths
and optimism of six-year-olds.

As you read in these pages about children's inherent strengths and positive attributes at every age level, it will become apparent that an overemphasis on standardized assessments shortchanges our children, whether in pre-kindergarten or eighth grade. It limits their opportunities to be deeply influenced by the skill and knowledge of and daily interaction with their teachers, and to build relationships and learning lessons in a community of scholars. I have spent over forty years in classrooms and schools where I have taught children, supervised as a principal, and supported as a coach. I know that the best teachers know their children individually, culturally, and developmentally at levels no standardized test can ever reach. You know in your parent or family conferences when you listen to such teachers that your children are learning lessons for the "right now" of childhood, lessons that excite them and motivate them, and that make them feel safe to take risks and make mistakes in pursuit of new knowledge.

This book is about your children, the ones in front of you right now at home and in the classroom. It is a catalog of their potential, their character, and the energy they hold to change the future. I hope *Yardsticks* will help you learn from, and learn about, these children.

Works Cited

Gesell, Arnold, and Beatrice Chandler Gesell. 1912. Preface to *The Normal Child and Primary Education*. New York: Ginn.

US Congress, Office of Technology Assessment. 1992. *Testing in American Schools: Asking the Right Questions*, OTA-SET-519. Washington, DC: Government Printing Office.

Introduction

For teachers, parents, and anyone else who wants to nurture the children in their lives, helping children grow starts with understanding where they are now. While every child is unique and develops at their own individual pace, development does follow some predictable patterns. And just as one measures a child's height with marks on a door jamb, year by year one can measure a child's physical, social, emotional, language, and cognitive development.

The primary goal of *Yardsticks* has not changed since it was first published in 1994: to provide teachers and parents with knowledge they can trust about how children grow and change. The book also continues to provide insight into children's cognitive curiosities and suggests appropriate teaching activities and approaches for each age, based on common developmental characteristics.

The observations and suggestions in *Yardsticks* reflect the particular cultural context of American schools, both in the United States and abroad. However, although *Yardsticks* does not specifically speak to the very different contexts in which teachers work and children grow in other countries, the developmental characteristics presented can be broadly useful throughout the world.

The developmental theories at the heart of *Yardsticks* are agreed upon by many researchers and field-tested by thousands of teachers. Year after year, we've heard from readers that this book has confirmed what they've observed on their own and has helped them make sense of those observations. And research completed in 2016 by Dr. Herbert M. Turner of ANALYTICA, Inc., and the University of Pennsylvania revealed that the book continues to depict very accurately how children and adolescents grow and how that growth often manifests itself in the classroom and at home.

With his research team, Dr. Turner surveyed teachers working in culturally diverse classrooms in urban, suburban, and rural schools, collectively teaching hundreds of students. The team's findings: a vast majority of teachers agree that the *Yardsticks* guidelines reflect what they typically see as they watch class after class of students move through the stages of development (Turner, Fleck, and Fu 2016).

Yardsticks grew out of the work of the *Responsive Classroom* approach, a developmentally attuned, evidence-based approach to teaching that offers practical strategies for bringing together academic and social-emotional learning throughout the school day. The approach is associated with greater teacher effectiveness, higher student achievement, and improved school climate, and is grounded in the belief that to teach children, we need to know them individually, culturally, and developmentally.

Since 1981, the *Responsive Classroom* approach has provided teachers with the resources to develop their skills in four critically important domains:

- Offering engaging academics
- Building a positive classroom and school community
- Effectively managing the classroom
- Creating conditions that are responsive to students' developmental strengths and needs

I encourage you to visit the *Responsive Classroom* website, www.responsiveclassroom.org, to learn more about the approach. However, you do not need to be implementing *Responsive Classroom* to benefit from reading and using the information presented in these pages. I hope that you'll come to rely on *Yardsticks* as thousands of teachers and parents before you have done to learn more about children's development and the strategies that work at different ages and stages of growth.

Most of all, I hope you'll keep in mind the captivating magic and mysteries of childhood and adolescence. As you do the hard daily work of nurturing and teaching the children in your life, take time also to appreciate the joys of noticing and celebrating their clear, honest vision—how they perceive and interact with the world at different stages of their growth. The overarching duty of all who care about children is to protect and nurture that vision. May *Yardsticks* support you in this undertaking.

Work Cited

Turner, Herb, Michael Fleck, and Rui Fu. 2016. "*Yardstick*'s Guidelines: What Research on Teachers Says." Organizational report. Turners Falls, MA: Center for Responsive Schools.

Learning More About Child Development

Teachers and parents wishing to deepen their knowledge of children's developmental characteristics might begin with classical Western child development works by researchers such as Jean Piaget, Arnold Gesell, Maria Montessori, Lev Vygotsky, Erik Erikson, Rudolph Steiner, Caroline Pratt, Lucy Sprague Mitchell, Dorothy Cohen, and Louise Bates Ames. Although written in the first half of the 20th century, these fundamental works continue to offer essential insights into how children grow and learn. Indeed, it is hard to imagine where our understanding of child development would be without them.

In the years since the classical theorists completed their research, our understanding of child development has been extended and enriched by succeeding generations of experts and by additional research. I especially recommend works by William Crain, Robert Pianta, Elena Bodrova, and Deborah J. Leong.

Of particular value in understanding the multicultural context of development in today's classrooms within American schools are works by James P. Comer, Sonia Nieto, Barbara Rogoff, Carol Ann Tomlinson, Beverly Daniel Tatum, and Sara Lawrence-Lightfoot.

To understand the exciting and dynamic field of brain research and its application to development and learning, please see works by Daniel J. Siegel, Daniel Goleman, Daniel Stern, and Louis Cozolino.

For more information, see the resource lists in Appendices A and B.

Knowing Our Students

Students go to school in many different types of communities, learn in a wide variety of classroom settings, and are taught by teachers using a broad and ever-changing array of curricula and methods. Yet one condition holds constant: To reach their fullest potential, students need teachers who know and understand them. Only when we know and understand our students can we build the relationships with them that allow us to provide the safe, supportive learning environments that enhance their growth and help them develop into happy, capable adults.

Knowing students means seeing them as whole people. We need to know not just how they do on tests and assignments but where they are developmentally. We also need to know something about each student's home culture, their dreams and concerns, and their unique personalities—and we need to understand how these elements intersect with the broad developmental stages that all children and adolescents experience.

Key Maxims of Child and Adolescent Development

Much of our knowledge of child and adolescent development comes from the work of psychologists and educators such as Jean Piaget, Beatrice and Arnold Gesell, Maria Montessori, Erik Erikson, and Lev Vygotsky. Over many years, these experts observed, researched, and documented how children change from age to age and discovered common patterns of growth.

These patterns vary somewhat in expression depending upon a variety of factors, including the culture in which children live. But physically, socially, emotionally, and cognitively, children and adolescents go through predictable stages of growth, during which they typically exhibit certain behavior patterns and develop particular capacities. Theorists differ to some extent in the way they describe the stages, but they generally agree about what happens during each one.

The accuracy of stage theory has been confirmed by later generations of researchers such as James P. Comer, Rachael Kessler, Sonia Nieto, and William Crain. It has also been confirmed by several generations of teachers and parents, whose close daily interactions with children and teens makes their observations extremely valuable.

These years of careful thought, research, and observation by researchers, teachers, and parents have given us a huge body of detailed information about childhood and adolescence, along with four universally observable maxims:

1. **Stages of growth and development follow a reasonably predictable pattern.** This can be seen in children's and adolescents' physical maturation, language acquisition, social and emotional behavior, cognition, and ways of approaching the world. For example, seven-year-olds are often more serious and cautious than six-year-olds, and twelve-year-olds tend to be gregarious explorers as they begin the journey into adolescence.

2. **Children and adolescents do not proceed through each stage at the same pace.** Although development is broadly similar the world over, important details are deeply influenced by culture, personality, and environment. Thus, individuals may go through predictable stages in the same order, but not necessarily at the same rate. Even within a single culture, if we compare two ten-year-olds, one child may be more like a typical nine-year-old developmentally while the other might begin to show an eleven-year-old's characteristics. This three-year developmental span around the chronological age is quite typical and is no cause for concern as long as each child's growth is relatively even and not delayed or erratic.

3. **Children and adolescents progress through the various aspects of development at their own rate.** One child might mature quickly in cognitive areas and slowly in physical and social ones, or vice versa. Others might develop capabilities in music, mechanical tasks, or graphic arts more quickly or slowly than language acquisition or the capability to perform academic tasks in school.

4. Growth is uneven. As children and adolescents pass through the stages of development, they tend to be more easygoing at some ages and more anxious or resistant at others. Cognitive growth seems to come in spurts followed by times of consolidation. Periods of obvious physical growth are often followed by periods of little noticeable change. This shifting back and forth is an integral part of the entire life cycle from childhood and adolescence, when changes are quite marked in both rate and degree, through adulthood and into the elder years.

Using these four principles as touchpoints for your teaching will help you understand what you're observing in the classroom, and will put into perspective the sometimes puzzling changes that play out as students grow. These principles will also enable you to make the best use of the information in the age-by-age guidelines (beginning on page 31) in order to reach students where they are and teach them in ways that will help them thrive.

Knowing Children and Adolescents Developmentally

As teachers, we calibrate our teaching by seeing how students do on tests and assignments; observing how they get along with classmates in partnerships, in large or small groups, on the bus and the playground, in the lunchroom, and during advisory or extracurricular activities; and noting how easily they move around the classroom and school, follow routines, and use materials and supplies. From these observations, we learn about students' strengths and areas of struggle. But we might still have questions:

Close observation and attention to detail are hallmarks of seven-year-olds. Note the placement of the sun.

Where is this individual (or group of students) developmentally? Is the behavior I'm seeing typical for this age? Understanding where students are developmentally will help you:

- Create a physical environment that matches developmental needs

- Structure appropriately challenging lessons

- Connect learning to students' strengths and interests

The *Yardsticks* age-by-age guidelines give detailed information about typical developmental characteristics in several areas. For ages four through ten, you'll learn about characteristics of physical development; social and emotional development; communication, language, and literacy; and cognitive capacity. For ages eleven through fourteen, you'll learn about characteristics in the areas of physical development; social and emotional development; cognitive capacity; ethics and self-direction; and moving toward independence. For all ages, you'll learn about how these characteristics relate to learning.

You'll get the best possible understanding of each student and each class by reading the guidelines for a three-year span: the age typically associated with the grade you teach, plus the ages below and above that age. For example, a third grade teacher would study the guidelines for eight-year-olds (the age typically associated with third grade) and also the guidelines for seven- and nine-year-olds.

The thinking behind this age-bracket strategy is twofold. First, as noted in the developmental maxims, chronological (or birthday) age and developmental age do not necessarily correlate directly, either physically, intellectually, emotionally, or socially. This means that in your seventh grade advisory, you might have a student who's chronologically twelve but more like a thirteen-year-old in some ways (in cognitive or language capabilities), more like an eleven-year-old in other ways (perhaps socially), and just like a typical twelve-year-old in still other ways (possibly in physical growth). Reading all three ages can help you understand behaviors or needs that seem inconsistent with what you usually expect from seventh graders.

The second reason for reviewing a three-year span of guidelines is that children in any one class are likely to span a range of chronological ages. For example, in a fourth grade class you might have a large group of children who are nine and a half. A few might be eight and just about to turn nine, and one or two might be ten. For this class, with many children in the second half of their ninth year, approaching ten, you'd want to be as familiar with the guidelines for ten-year-olds as with those for nine-year-olds and adjust your teaching accordingly. To learn more about assessing the overall developmental age of your class, see Appendix C, "The Birthday Cluster Exercise."

As you look at the students you teach through the lens of the information in the age-by-age sections, it's important to keep in mind that these are guidelines, not rules. Knowing students developmentally is just one piece of the puzzle. As developmental maxim #2 notes, each individual's passage through the stages of development is influenced by other factors as well, and to truly know students, we also need to know them personally and culturally.

Knowing Students Personally— Taking the Time to Observe and Listen

Knowing students personally means taking the time to truly see each individual. And a good first step is to simply observe and listen to them. In the classroom, during lunchroom and recess duty, as they enter the classroom and settle in, as you move with them about the school, and while they wait in line, you have many opportunities to focus for a few moments on one student at a time.

You can take note of whom the student works and socializes with, what they talk about when they're free to talk about anything, which lessons they respond to with excitement and enthusiasm, when during the day their energy is lowest and highest, and when they seem unusually happy or sad.

Knowing students in this way—knowing their personalities, passions, anxieties—will help you make sense of how they are navigating their current developmental stage.

How Well Are You Seeing?

A simple but powerful way to discover how well you're seeing students and letting them know they're seen is by using this exercise devised by educator and author Donald Graves.

1. Divide a piece of paper into three columns.

2. In the first column, quickly write the names of your students in the order in which they come to mind.

3. In the second column, next to each name, write one thing you know about that student that doesn't have anything to do with school. This might be a fact about their "outside" life, something they like to do, or something they care passionately about: "Grandma lives with the family," "On the town softball team," "Wants to save sea creatures."

4. Finally, in the third column, put a star or a check mark if you're sure they know that you're aware of this fact about them.

If it took you awhile to remember certain names for the first column, you may want to observe these students more often and make sure you call them by name whenever you speak to them.

If you found it tough to come up with a fact to write in the second column, more observation and listening will help. Talk with the student at recess or breaks, schedule a private lunch or book chat, or send a note home asking parents to share insights about the student's talents and interests.

When your third column shows students who probably don't realize you're aware of important personal details about them, look for moments when you can comment on or ask questions about things you know are important to them.

Name	Something I know about this child that is not school related	I'm sure this child knows I'm aware of this
Marta	Kicked a goal in soccer last weekend	✓
Johnny	Likes to act; is going to be in a play	
Sanjay	Is learning to play the ukulele	✓

Thirteen-year-olds often feel the fragility of growing into adolescence, depicted here as different flowers doing a tentative dance together.

Knowing Students Culturally

We teach in increasingly diverse classrooms. Students differ from each other not just in racial, ethnic, and national origins but also in income level, family structure, spiritual or religious beliefs, traditions, etiquette, career expectations, and many other parameters.

This rich diversity matters to educators because culture mediates how students experience the universal stages of development, how they see the world of school, and how they learn best. And culture—our own as well as that of the students we teach—also influences our assessment of their cognitive, social, and emotional development.

Consider, for example, a student from a family in which speaking out in public is discouraged. Without an understanding of that cultural norm, we might think their reluctance to speak in front of the class means they don't understand the content or concept we're teaching. Or we might assume that their social skills are lagging behind those of others their age. Once we understand the behavior from the student's cultural perspective, we can adjust our teaching to best support their learning—perhaps inviting them to show what they've learned in nonverbal (or at least nonpublic) ways and doing some extra scaffolding of their speaking skills.

Here are some things to keep in mind as you get to know students culturally.

1. **Think in terms of differences, not deficits.** Cultural differences are just that—different ways of looking at and being in the world, not problems or flaws. Thinking of the range of needs, strengths, and learning styles in your classroom as differences rather than deficits allows you to adapt your teaching to meet these varied learning styles.

2. **Be aware of your own cultural viewpoint.** We all have an implicit cultural bias. For example, if you've ever visited a state or country where people spoke English with an accent different from yours, you may have been surprised to learn that they thought *you* had an accent. In the same way, the ideas and values of the culture we grew up in are so tightly woven into our way of being that we may not even realize we have a cultural viewpoint. Instead, it's easy to assume that our beliefs and practices reflect the way things really are or should be for everyone, everywhere.

By examining—kindly and without judgment—the source of your beliefs about how students should learn and behave, what families should look like, and so on, you'll be better able to "hear how you sound" and "see how you see." Understanding that your own cultural framework is just one of many ways of looking at the world will help you clearly see the students before you, treat their cultural experiences as equally valid, and teach them with respect and understanding.

3. **Think broadly about diversity.** In a sense, if the cultural background of just one student you teach differs from your own or that of their peers, you teach in a culturally plural environment. Understanding diversity in this way lets you see beyond group identity ("the class") and respond with sensitivity and empathy to the needs of each student.

4. **Hold close the conviction that all students, from all cultures, can learn and want to learn.** This belief will help you maintain the same high expectations for all, which is a key component of educational equity, and will help you provide choices for and pathways to learning that will support success for all students in your classroom.

5. **Learn about students' cultures.** The more you know about a student's culture, the better prepared you'll be to interact with them and their families in ways they find comfortable and respectful. For every student in your class, try to be aware of:

  ◆ *Nonverbal communication behaviors,* such as how far to stand from someone you're speaking to.

- *Conversational norms,* such as how to bring up sensitive topics.

- *Values related to learning,* which may affect, among other things, how parents support their children. For example, do parents praise children's accomplishments, or do they refrain from doing so because they believe children should learn to be self-effacing?

- *Cultural learning styles.* Some cultures learn and transfer information primarily through reading and writing; others have strong oral traditions in which information is passed from person to person through stories, proverbs, songs, conversations, and other forms of speech.

- *Cultural mindset.* Where does a student's family or culture fall on the individualism–collectivism continuum? Individualistic cultures emphasize self-reliance and individual choice, achievement, and independence; collectivist cultures emphasize cooperative learning, the well-being of the group, and the importance of relationships.

- *The culture's contributions* to science, politics, literature, the arts, and other areas. Your discoveries will provide insight into the culture's values and perspectives and the richness the student brings to the classroom.

6. **Use culturally relevant teaching practices.** To make learning as accessible as possible for all students, think about adaptations you can make to classroom practice. For example:

- *Use active (hands-on) learning.* Games focused on academic content, as well as brief, energizing movement breaks in between lessons, capture students' attention and require their active engagement. Because most games require verbal communication, they can tap into oral traditions and learning styles shared by many cultures.

◆ *Use interactive (social) learning.* Social interaction fosters cognitive growth, gives students opportunities to be known, and lets them bring their cultural perspectives into their learning. Activities that include interaction also let students learn from one another while strengthening the classroom community.

◆ *Use stories.* Virtually all cultures value storytelling in some form. Telling and writing stories strengthens learning across the curriculum by helping students make sense of, share, and remember what they've learned. Storytelling also lets students share about themselves and their culture while building vocabulary and developing their facility in using literary devices such as alliteration, repetition, and metaphor.

7. **Look to parents as resources** in getting to know their children. As the experts on their child and their home environment, parents can help you understand how family values, child-raising practices, and expectations might translate into the student's behavior and needs at school.

If connecting and talking openly with parents seems difficult, keep in mind that their relationship with school may differ dramatically from what you've learned to expect within your own culture. For example, in some cultures it's considered insulting to educators for parents to offer advice or suggestions about how to teach their child. Some parents may feel uncomfortable because their own early experiences with school were

Frequent conversations and reflection with different partners builds a capacity for empathy and appreciation of different points of view.

negative; others may worry that they don't speak English well enough to talk meaningfully with you.

It's best to assume that all parents care very much about their child's education and will become willing partners when you find comfortable ways for them to do so. Your school, district, or community may have a family engagement counselor who can offer suggestions and support.

Be a Seeing Teacher

As you work with the developmental guidelines in this book, I hope you'll come back to this chapter now and then. Use it as a reminder of the power of understanding the developmental patterns of your students as they grow, and know that taking the time to observe what students are doing and how they are learning is the best formative assessment of all.

Use it, too, as a reminder of the power of your profession, of the broad array of knowledge and skills you use to teach every student, every day, and of the way you strive to tune your teaching to their developmental, personal, and cultural needs.

And finally, use this chapter as a reminder of the importance of knowing the students you teach as distinct individuals. For you can make the most of your teaching skills and your developmental knowledge only when you turn your eyes, mind, and heart to seeing all students, in all their fullness and complexity, for the unique people they are and the people they are becoming before your eyes.

About the Term "Parent"

Students come from homes with a variety of family structures. Students might be raised by grandparents, siblings, aunts and uncles, foster families, and other caregivers. All of these individuals are to be honored for devoting their time, attention, and love to raising children.

It's difficult to find one word that encompasses all these caregivers. In this book, for ease of reading, we use the term "parent" to represent all the caregivers involved in a child's life.

Getting the Most Out of *Yardsticks*

In order for students to succeed in and out of school, they need to develop both social-emotional and academic competencies. They need to know how to cooperate, assert themselves respectfully, and take responsibility for their actions. They need to develop empathy and self-control. Academically, along with developing strategies that will help them actively learn content and contribute to the learning community, they need a mindset that values growth and an ability to persevere even when tasks are difficult.

Understanding where students are developmentally—what their growth patterns and typical capacities are at each age—will help teachers and parents nurture and support them as they grow and learn.

Overview of the Age-by-Age Guidelines

The age-by-age "yardsticks," or guidelines, which begin on page 31, are designed to give you insight into children's developmental characteristics and how those characteristics may affect their experiences at school and at home. This overview will help you get the greatest possible benefit from the guidelines as you use them to teach or parent children at each age and stage of development.

OPENING NARRATIVE

Each age section opens with a description that highlights what's intriguing, delightful, and sometimes challenging about that age. I encourage you to read these to get an overall feel for the age's characteristics and the wonders and complexities of being a child.

INFORMATION FOR PARENTS

At the beginning of each age section, set off in a box, parents will find helpful developmental information specific to that age that relates to the child at home.

THE GUIDELINES

The developmental information for each age is sorted into two broad categories.

Typical growth patterns: These are the typical behaviors and needs you can expect to see at each age, along with information on the ways these behaviors and needs shape how students work and play in school.

For children ages 4–10, these growth patterns are further broken down into physical development; social and emotional development; communication, language, and literacy; and cognitive capacity.

For adolescents ages 11–14, the subcategories are somewhat different to emphasize the growing sense of self and the importance of peer group: physical development; social and emotional development; cognitive capacity; ethics and self-direction; and moving toward independence.

How the growth patterns relate to learning: This category offers suggestions for age-appropriate tasks and materials in the specific areas of reading, writing, and math as well as across the curriculum (including social studies, languages, science, and special areas). This development-centered approach to teaching will help ensure that every child comes to love learning, creativity, and problem-solving for their own sake, while also enabling children to hone their academic skills and their knowledge of content areas.

Reading highlights opportunities that will help students develop their reading skills to the fullest. For example, in the section for seven-year-olds, you'll see that they'll benefit from intense phonics instruction in small groups and that independent reading becomes increasingly important from age seven on. If you teach twelve-year-olds, you'll see that they enjoy nonfiction reading tied to subjects that interest them.

Writing highlights skills students are ready to use. Nine- year-olds, for example, can tackle descriptive writing, character development, plot, cohesiveness, and believability. Fourteen-year-olds can write across genres and experiment with writing in different

Fourteen-year-olds thrive when they can choose how to represent learning, using their unique talents and strengths.

voices. This category also covers what students typically like to write about and their capabilities in spelling.

Math highlights activities that are especially effective in helping students develop their math capabilities. Complicated word problems, for example, are excellent for eleven-year-olds, and all ages thrive on math activities relating to the real world. For very young children, such activities might include counting and measuring objects in the classroom or at home.

Across the curriculum highlights opportunities that will help students develop both social-emotional and academic skills in all subject areas and in special area classrooms. For example, you'll learn that six-year-olds relish experimenting with new tools and learning new skills, and that eight-year-olds have a growing interest in how things work and enjoy learning about the natural world through nonfiction reading in science and social studies.

As you explore this information, please remember that chronological age and cognitive growth do not necessarily go hand in hand. Some students, for instance, will be ready for reading instruction at an early age, whereas others may be ready only after they've passed the typical age. The same holds true for readiness across the curriculum.

On the other hand, waiting too long for children to be ready for instruction, especially in reading, writing, or math, can be detrimental to their growth. With reading, for example, intervention is essential if children are not engaging with the reading curriculum and developing basic skills during their first grade year.

Many schools do diagnostic work around both reading and math capabilities at the beginning, middle, and end of kindergarten and first grade. These diagnostic check-ins are immensely helpful, yet for knowing what each child needs and when, nothing will ever replace the day-to-day observances of "seeing teachers."

Tips for Using the *Yardsticks* Guidelines

Both parents and teachers can use the guidelines in this book to understand what's happening with a particular child right now, or to look ahead with an eye to planning how they might respond to needs and behaviors that are likely on the horizon.

FOR TEACHERS

Following are suggestions for ways teachers might use these guidelines:

- Better understand each student and each year's group of students

- Consider or reconsider how to group students for seat work or activities

- Overhaul the classroom's physical organization so that it better accommodates students' developmental capabilities to navigate through space without bumping into things (or people)

- Gather fresh ideas for planning lessons or choosing read-aloud books on the basis of capabilities, needs, and interests

- Adjust expectations, lesson plans, classroom organization, and ways of relating to students as they grow during the year and begin to show the developmental characteristics typically associated with the next chronological age

- Initiate a discussion, especially with older students, of what is considered typical for that age and whether it rings true for them

Following are suggestions for ways parents might use these guidelines:

- ◆ Evaluate how the curriculum and classroom life seem to fit their child's needs

- ◆ Better understand their child's behavior at school

- ◆ Better understand their child's behavior at home (which, at certain ages, tends to differ from behavior at school)

The most important thing of all to keep in mind as you use these guidelines is that each student is an individual: Their development will be unique even though it fits within broad developmental patterns. With that truth in mind, the guidelines in this book are offered not as standards to live up to, but as general indicators to help guide teachers and parents in understanding child and adolescent growth.

A Word About Technology

The use of technology has become common in many classrooms, often beginning in the early grades. Keeping in mind the developmental stages of the students you teach, here are some general guidelines to follow when introducing and using technological tools in the classroom.

Teach, model, practice. As with any classroom tool or resource, teach students the routines necessary for safe and productive use of technology, and then practice those routines. For younger students, such routines might be as basic as how to turn devices on and off and how to care for them. If students will use computers or tablets for standardized testing, be sure they know how to navigate around the devices. For older students, additional routines might include safe and appropriate use of a wide range of applications and techniques for building websites, creating podcasts, making movies, designing presentations, and carrying out productive online research.

Use technology with purpose. Technology is a tool for students just as manipulatives and art supplies are. And as with any tool you choose, technology should enhance learning, build the classroom community, and make learning active and interactive.

Keep technology use safe. Even students who are adept at using technology will need your guidance in how to use it safely and productively. Know your school's policy on technology use and teach it to students.

Monitor students' use. As students gain independence with using technology, you'll need to stay actively involved. Circulate, check in, and when needed, remind them of established routines and rules. Have regular discussions about technology use: What has been successful? What has been challenging?

Connect classroom or school rules to use of digital media. Facebook, Snapchat, Instagram, texting apps, YouTube, Twitter—students have around-the-clock access to digital media, and the use—and abuse—of this media can have an impact on the classroom community. Take the time to talk about expectations for use of digital media and how classroom or school rules apply to media use.

Four-year-olds love learning to work together.

Four-Year-Olds

"Give me my Bunny!" he said.
"You mustn't say that. He isn't a toy. He's REAL!"

The Velveteen Rabbit ✳ by Margery Williams

When my son was four years old, we lived on a paved country road that saw occasional but speedy traffic. One Saturday morning, a worried motorist knocked on the door. "Do you have a little boy and a dog? If you do, they're a half mile up the road and moving fast." The yard gate had been opened by the boy's intelligent fingers for the first time and boy and dog had made their escape into the world. Fortunately, we retrieved them safely, changed the gate lock, and continued our education of, and by, the four-year-old.

—*Chip Wood*

Fours tend to be ready for everything. They are explorers and adventurers who are soaking up the world of knowledge with incredible speed. Capable of almost nonstop mental and physical gymnastics, they throw themselves into nearly every activity with enthusiasm and a sense of purpose.

Four-year-olds are flexible, exciting, and creative creatures who love to exaggerate and engage in imaginative play. A four-year-old's tall tale about an adventure she had with an imaginary friend may puzzle a parent or teacher but delight the four-year-old. And this play is critical for the development of fours' understanding of right and wrong, early application of social rules, and manners. They sometimes can seem especially "bossy" (particularly with their real and imaginary friends), but this assertiveness is positive rehearsal for learning acceptable limits and how to be a real friend and helper.

Fours also respond joyfully to outdoor play. They seem drawn to the horizon and love to run and ride, pull, dig, and climb. Parents and teachers need plenty of energy to keep up with these young dynamos.

Vocabulary expands rapidly at four—nonsense words, rhyming words, unacceptable words, gigantic words, words that grown-ups say, nonsense babble that babies say, sounds that animals make, imaginary languages that fairies speak.

In fact, everything about four-year-olds signals rapid development. Just as they're growing taller and frequently needing new clothes and shoes, they're also trying on and taking off different personalities, roles, and interests. They do this with an amazing sense of imagination and humor. They're as interested in playing grown-up roles of doctors and firefighters, mommies and daddies, dancers and soldiers as they are in portraying fairies and princes, lions and tigers, superheroes and monsters.

They like feeling independent, but when they want adult help they want it eagerly and immediately: a push on the swing, a snack, help with making a letter look right, someone to play with them. They look up to the adults in their lives, and teachers

4-Year-Olds at Home

- Can make choices on their own but appreciate adult input and suggestions
- Need help expressing needs with words rather than actions—reminders to "use your words" are helpful
- Love to have "jobs" such as setting the table or folding clothes
- Are sometimes fearful or worried, especially older fours, and may have nightmares or trouble sleeping; regular bedtime routines are helpful
- Love being read to

Fours learn best through their own play;
learning goes from hand to head.

and parents can see and hear themselves mirrored in four-year-olds' movements, their gestures and facial expressions, and their tones of voice and choices of words.

Fours learn best through their own play—by acting out stories and fairy tales, expressing themselves with visual art materials, and manipulating clay, building blocks, and math materials. This is an age when much learning is transmitted through the large muscles, when learning goes from the hand to the head, not the other way around. The implications for the classroom teacher are to minimize paper-and-pencil tasks and provide opportunities for imaginative play and movement throughout the classroom and outside.

Typical Growth Patterns of 4-Year-Olds

PHYSICAL DEVELOPMENT

◆ Visual focus is on faraway objects; have trouble with close visual activities, such as reading and writing

◆ Can't switch smoothly between near and far focus; have a hard time copying from the board

◆ Fine motor skills not well developed yet; awkward with writing, handcrafts, and other small movements

◆ Learn more through large muscle activity and constructive play, such as stacking large blocks, than through desktop paper-and-pencil activities

◆ Often clumsy; collisions and spills are common; teaching cleanup techniques supports independence

◆ Energetic and active; need time for running, jumping, climbing, and dancing

SOCIAL AND EMOTIONAL DEVELOPMENT

◆ Friendly, talkative, "bubbly"; love being with friends, though they still often work near, not with, a friend

◆ Love learning to work together; "Who's the boss?" is often a major developmental issue; can learn basic turn-taking skills, but the teacher saying "It's the rule" works wonders, too

CONTINUED ▶

◆ Not overly dependent on adults and can make choices based on their own interests; usually make good use of adult suggestions

◆ Need adult help finding words to express needs instead of reacting physically; teacher language is very important in helping children use language instead of physical means: "Use words," "Tell her what you want," "Ask if he is finished," etc.

◆ Easily redirected from inappropriate behavior (for example, to a youngster rushing for the stairs: "Jessie, stop!"); need teacher redirection and modeling of appropriate behavior and chances to practice ("Now go down the stairs safely—watch how I do it, then you try")

◆ Small dramas and role-plays led by the teacher help teach social skills (for example, how to take turns)

◆ Love school "jobs," such as taking attendance or putting out snack

COMMUNICATION, LANGUAGE, LITERACY

◆ Very talkative

◆ Imaginative; love dress-up and drama; enjoy experimenting with language, delighting in big words, long explanations, bathroom language, and swear words

◆ Enjoy being read to, whether individually, in small groups, or as a whole class; love to do their own "reading" of picture books

Fours need to move! They stretch their minds when they stretch their bodies—and they have fun following directions.

COGNITIVE CAPACITY

◆ Have short attention spans; move quickly from one thing to another; hard for them to stay in one area of the classroom for an extended time

◆ Learn best by moving large muscles; need to play and explore

◆ Can learn responsibilities that are carefully taught, such as room cleanup at the end of a work period, but need the teacher to model expectations

◆ Constantly reading their environment; labeling objects that children frequently see or use gives them many opportunities to practice

READING

Provide opportunities for children this age to:

◆ Be read to, especially from picture books with repetitive words

◆ Be storytellers as well as listeners, working together in a small group with a teacher or assistant to sequence events in a familiar story or change the story to add their ideas

◆ Do "parallel" reading with an adult: The child "reads" one page of a familiar book (tells the story while looking at the words and pictures), and the adult reads the next

◆ Build the sequences of reading by listening to or parallel reading books with repeating phrases and few words, or pictures and no words

---

WRITING

Expect from these children:

◆ **Writing** Very little paper-and-pencil work focused only on mechanical skills; instead fours benefit from a focus on building early literacy skills through scribbling and using invented spelling

◆ **Writing themes** Fascination with blood and gore, fantasy, TV takeoffs, fairy tales, and pets

◆ **Handwriting** Mainly scribble writing and drawing; typically grasp pencil in whole fist and use their arm, hand, and fingers as a single unit; young fours may hold pencil more tentatively toward the eraser and write with a very light stroke; older fours write more boldly and firmly; printing is usually large

◆ **Beginning spelling** Prephonemic—many letters do not correspond to sounds; for example, they might write or say "B-H-K-E-E-E-E-E-E-J-B" for sailboat

MATH

Provide opportunities for children this age to:

◆ Learn through hands-on experiences with manipulatives such as magnets, pulleys, puzzles, interlocking cubes, scoops, funnels, measuring cups, and sand

◆ Practice counting through "real" jobs such as taking attendance and doing the milk count; job charts make it easy for children to check items off and tally

◆ Explore math through stories: How many monkeys jumping on the bed this time?

ACROSS THE CURRICULUM
(including social studies, languages, science, special areas)

Provide opportunities for children this age to:

◆ Improve communication skills through imaginative play, such as on a puppet stage or in a dress-up corner

◆ Paint at stand-up easels with easy access to drying racks or clothesline hang-ups for finished paintings; this supports development of large motor skills and the ability to visually represent learning in age-appropriate ways

◆ Use climbing apparatus on the playground; do tumbling activities in PE

◆ Get ready for writing by practicing with finger paints, chubby pencils, colored chalk on playgrounds

◆ Take part in organized recess games with an adult or older student leader

◆ Engage in activities that use music, rhythm, and repeating patterns

Four-year-olds' drawings often show complex thinking;
ask what a drawing represents and be ready for a surprise.
Fine motor skills are still developing.

Five-year-olds love challenging themselves on the playground as well as in the classroom.

Five-Year-Olds

"Ramona loved Miss Binney so much she did not want to disappoint her. Not ever. Miss Binney was the nicest teacher in the whole world."

Ramona the Pest ✳ by Beverly Cleary

After a busy morning in an overly academic kindergarten, a five-year-old boy marched up to his teacher's desk, put his hands on his hips, and announced, "You don't seem to understand, teacher; I just came here to eat and play!"

—*Sue Sweitzer*
Trainer, Gesell Institute

Oh, what fun to be five! This year is, overall, a time of great happiness for children. Life is "good!" say the five-year-olds as they take on the adventure of each brand-new day. They're consolidating the rapid growth of the previous year, becoming calmer, more literal and exact, and more attuned to details as they rest from the wild exuberance of four. Yet, they still see every corner of the classroom and home as full of possibilities for exploring, doing, and imagining.

Five-year-olds take in the world through their senses. They see, smell, touch, hear, and taste just about everything—one thing after another, but only one thing at a time. Their intense focus on detail enables them to see not just the butterfly but the pattern on its wings, its proboscis uncurling into a flower, its antennae waving delicately. Fives can give sustained attention to anything that fascinates them. They'll squat down quietly to watch that butterfly for as long as it pauses in flight. For twenty minutes or even half an hour or more, they'll busy themselves in creating imaginative worlds in which they feel safe and engaged.

Learning is at its best for fives when it is both structured and exploratory: structured through a clear and predictable schedule, exploratory through carefully constructed areas where they can initiate their own active discoveries through play—the vital work of the five-year-old.

Although fives are just beginning to learn empathy and still see things primarily from their own point of view, social relationships matter very much to them. They love exploring the "real world" with other fives by making believe they're teachers, moms, dads, astronauts, or firefighters. Dressing up and playing with puppets add to the fun.

Like Ramona in the opening quote, fives adore and care a great deal about pleasing significant adults. They constantly ask, "Can I help mow the lawn? Can I feed the puppy? Can I use these markers? Is this how you do it? How much paper can I use?" Fives expect and need adults to create safe boundaries and tell them what is happening next, where they're going, and whether

5-Year-Olds at Home

- ◆ Need lots of physical activity but can usually pace themselves and rest before they get too tired

- ◆ Want adult approval when newly five but may begin to challenge adults as they move toward six

- ◆ Respond well to routines and clear expectations

- ◆ Appreciate guided choices that allow them to make decisions for themselves

- ◆ Often answer "good" to general questions, such as "How was school today?"; will respond in more detail to specific questions, such as "You had music class today, right? What did you do? What was most fun?"

they're there yet. They need permission from adults to move from one task or activity to the next and usually accept adult rules as absolute and unbendable.

As they move through their fifth year, many children begin a growth spurt and become ever more ready to take on their widening world with growing self-confidence. Older fives may test the rules at home and at school, stretch themselves to see what they can do on their own, and sometimes stretch the truth. They begin to care more about figuring things out for themselves than about getting answers (and behavior) exactly right—a main focus when they were just a bit younger.

Teachers and parents can best support older fives by inviting their input and offering them guided choices. Thus, "How long do you think you'll need to finish your journal page?" often works better at school than "You have five minutes to finish that page in your journal." At home, "Would you like to finish picking up your clothes before or after snack?" speaks to the five-year-old's need to make decisions for themselves.

Truly, though, such adult sensitivity and responsiveness to their changing needs is essential to all fives (and to all children). When we give five-year-olds clear and simple expectations and choices, offer plenty of time to play, marvel with them at the world, and tune in to the wonder of their changing minds and bodies, they can grow into joyous inventors, creators, and problem-solvers, at school and in life.

Typical Growth Patterns of 5-Year-Olds

PHYSICAL DEVELOPMENT

◆ Still developing left-to-right visual tracking essential for reading fluency; may focus on one word at a time and read haltingly; finding the first word in a next line can sometimes be difficult, and they often need to use a pointer or finger to keep their place

◆ Reverse letters and numbers, either swapping positions, as in writing "ot" for "to," or drawing the letters themselves backward so that a "d" looks like a "b"; to help children become more self-aware, teachers can ask about the letter they reversed but not ask them to correct the reversal

◆ Find it hard to space letters, numbers, and words; using a finger as a separator helps

◆ Visual focus is on objects close at hand; still have difficulty copying from the board

◆ Need lots of physical activity; love indoor and outdoor physical play and activity, including lively games such as Duck, Duck, Goose and Red Light, Green Light

◆ Better control of running, jumping, and other large movements

◆ Staying focused in structured gym class can be difficult

◆ Often fall or slip out of chairs sideways

◆ Usually pace themselves well; will generally rest before they're exhausted

CONTINUED ▶

- May prefer to work standing up; some schools are now providing some stand-up desk spaces

- Still awkward with writing, handcrafts, and tasks requiring small movements

- Hold pencils with three-fingered, pincer-like grasp; may need pencil grip to help them relax

- Ready to begin learning manuscript printing; not always able to stay within lines

SOCIAL AND EMOTIONAL DEVELOPMENT

- Young fives depend on adult authority and want adult approval; like to help, cooperate, follow rules, and be "good"; love having jobs to do in the classroom

- Older fives may challenge adult authority and seem oppositional at times

- Want verbal permission from adults; can pace themselves while doing a given task but may need to be released to move from task to task; before acting, will ask "Can I . . . ?"

- Need consistent routines, rules, and discipline; respond well to clear and simple expectations, such as "I will always ring the chime just once, which means put down what's in your hands and look at me"

- Can sit and work at quiet activities for fifteen to twenty minutes at a time, particularly tasks with manipulatives such as pretend or real money, counting cubes, attribute blocks, and other concrete objects

COMMUNICATION, LANGUAGE, LITERACY

- Use and interpret words in their literal or most basic sense; unable to think abstractly; "We're late—we've got to fly!" means "We've got to take to the air like birds!"

- Younger fives express themselves in few words; "play" and "good" are favorites

- More complex in their imaginative expression than fours; like to express themselves through words, drawing, and drama

- Often read aloud even when asked to read silently

- Older fives like to explain things and have things explained to them; will often give elaborate answers to questions

COGNITIVE CAPACITY

- Have a developing sense of time; don't clearly know what "five minutes" or "in a little while" means; respond well to use of a sand timer where they can see time passing

- Often see only one way to do things; rarely see things from another's viewpoint

CONTINUED ▶

◆ Not ready to understand abstract concepts such as "fairness"; the teacher will have to provide lots of examples as the year progresses: "Each one of you gets the help you need to learn new things—this is how I will be fair to everyone in our class-room"

◆ Imagination can be vivid, which can lead to believing toys and other objects are actually alive

◆ Learn best and express thoughts through active play, repetition, copying, and hands-on exploration of materials such as manipulatives, clay, sand, and water

◆ Think intuitively rather than logically; for example, "It's windy when the trees shake, so the trees must make the wind"

◆ Like to copy and to repeat stories, poems, songs, and games, sometimes with minor variations; enjoy sets of similar math and science tasks

◆ Can become stuck in repetitive behavior (for example, always drawing rainbows or flowers) for fear of making mistakes when trying something new

◆ May still "talk their thoughts" out loud; for example, saying "I'm going to move the truck!" before doing so (more typical at four)

◆ Do best learning with predictable daily schedules reviewed each morning and carried out with a minimum of transitions; need clear routines for these transitions; as much as possible make sure that key events in the day, such as snack, art, and closing circle, happen in the same place, at the same time

READING

Provide opportunities for children this age to:

- Vocalize while they read or read out loud quietly to themselves, rather than being expected to do sustained, silent reading

- Do "partner" reading—peers helping each other through familiar books; more able readers may pair well with more beginning readers, but both need to play an active role (as in "parallel" reading)

- Have short chapter books read to them sometimes by readers from older classrooms

- Write stories or reports with a partner or small group of class-mates and turn them into books for the classroom library

- Strengthen their reading skills by reading predictable books (books with few words, much repetition, and many pictures)

- Learn phonics in small groups with children at similar skill levels

- Create labels, signs, posters, and charts identifying familiar objects in their environment, such as areas of the room, use of shelves, etc.

WRITING

Expect from these children:

◆ **Writing** Labeling of drawings with initial consonants or vowels to stand for one feature in the drawing (as in "H" for "house" in a drawing of houses, people, and trees); tell stories in a single drawing and one or two words

◆ **Beginning spelling** Largely prephonemic or early phonemic— beginning to use initial consonants or vowels to represent words and sometimes stringing those initial letters together in "sentences" such as I STBFL (I see the butterfly)

◆ **Writing themes** Family, family trips, fairy tales, tales of good and evil, stories about pets, and stories about themselves and best friends

◆ **Handwriting** Switch to three-fingered pencil grasp; tendency to write only uppercase letters; as understanding of spelling develops, use of irregular spacing between words

---

MATH

Provide opportunities for children this age to:

◆ Count and sort, make sets, do simple addition and subtraction using real materials, and make graphs with stickers or cut-out pictures to represent such things as favorite ice cream, games they love to play, or number of siblings in their family

◆ Practice writing numbers

- Do simple equations, such as "What's the missing number?" $(5 - ? = 2)$

- Continue hands-on exploration of size, shape, length, and volume

---

ACROSS THE CURRICULUM
(including social studies, languages, science, special areas)

Provide opportunities for children this age to:

- Take risks and try new things through teacher-structured "daily challenges," such as drawing a forest without flowers or drawing a rainbow vertically on the page; ask them for ideas as well

- Take part in active structured playground games in PE, at recess, or in the regular classroom

- Practice making controlled small movements through simple activities such as weaving, tying shoes, and tracing mazes

- Learn and practice language skills through teacher modeling, directed role-play, and dramatic play

- View and draw simple three-dimensional blocks or shapes from different sitting positions to help them see things from different points of view

Six-year-olds approach both work and play with delight.

Six-Year-Olds

"But now I am six, I'm as clever as clever.
So I think I'll be six now for ever and ever."

"The End," *Now We Are Six* ✳ by A. A. Milne

One of my favorite children's books about school is *First Grade Takes a Test* by Miriam Cohen. In this book, the children are confounded by the experience of taking a timed test for the first time. They have to keep still, answer questions without help from their friends, and finish within a specified period of time. Several hilarious examples of six-year-old thinking show that sixes are not at all ready for formal testing. Here's my favorite:

"On the test there was a picture of Sally and Tom. Sally was giving Tom something. It looked like a bologna sandwich. Underneath it said:

☐ Sally is taller than Tom.
☐ Tom is taller than Sally.

Jim wondered what being tall had to do with getting a bologna sandwich. And was it really a bologna sandwich? It might be tomato . . . Jim took a long time on that one."

—*Chip Wood*

Curious. Eager. Industrious. Enthusiastic. Imaginative. These words barely hint at the wonderful liveliness and excitement about the world that define children's sixth year. It's a time of dramatic physical, cognitive, and social change, a time of intense receptivity to all new learning that is perhaps never again matched at any other period in the human lifespan.

At six, children's capacity for logical thought begins to blossom. As in Piaget's classic experiment, a six-year-old will tell you that two equal balls of clay remain equal in volume even when one is rolled out into a snake shape. Sixes also begin to grasp cause and effect in the natural world, understanding, for example, that it's the wind that makes the trees move, not vice versa.

This growing capacity for understanding extends to social relationships. Whereas fives are the center of their own universe, not yet able to see things from another person's perspective, sixes begin to understand other points of view and can consider rules and behavior with greater objectivity. Playmates and classmates become as important as parents and teachers, and six-year-olds delight in cooperative projects, activities, and tasks.

Children's rapid physical growth during this year is mirrored in rapid physical activity. Classrooms full of six-year-olds are—and need to be—busy, noisy places that reflect the "in a hurry" nature of being six. Humming, whistling, and bustling are the order of the day, and with their rapidly expanding vocabularies, sixes live in an out-loud world of constant and contagious talk. They have so much to tell each other, as well as the grown-ups!

Children now approach schoolwork and spontaneous play with equal delight; no job is too big, no mountain too high. They race through tasks, assignments, and games; it's quantity more than quality, process rather than product that count for sixes—along with trying new things. They love being first to read a new book, spell a new word, or make a new friend (although if they can't be first, they may gladly dawdle, trying to be last). The six-year-old's love of novelty extends to classroom and at-home tasks, which they accept joyfully—as long as assignments change frequently. Paradoxically, though, they prefer the same comforting bedtime routine night after night.

Any adventure or activity that invites exploration, discovery, asking questions, sharing thoughts, and explaining what they know will engage six-year-olds. They love to be outdoors, whether to learn a game, play at recess, go on a field trip, or check on the weather. They also delight in indoor fun, such as silly jokes, goofy songs, and guessing games.

Treats and surprises from parents and teachers also delight these exuberant children. Notes in lunchboxes, special messages from teachers—these are treated as wonders each time they appear. In fact, as six-year-olds work hard to understand and order the world in new ways, such adult encouragement from home and school will support the blossoming balance between dependence on adults and increasing independent confidence.

Sixes are always on the lookout for partners and friends to work with. This child may have created a "fish friend" for herself.

6-Year-Olds at Home

- ◆ Tire easily and may experience frequent illness—collaborate with teachers on creating a schoolwork activity bag for those times when children miss school due to illness

- ◆ Like to take on increased responsibility and appreciate having choices in household chores

- ◆ Thrive on encouragement and are easily upset when criticized

- ◆ Can be strongly affected by events at school; bedtime may be a good time to ask about something that seems to be worrying your child; listening is more important than giving advice

Typical Growth Patterns of 6-Year-Olds

PHYSICAL DEVELOPMENT

◆ More aware of their fingers as tools; can use their fingers to count on, trace a maze, maneuver electronic devices, balance a scale, pour exact amounts

◆ Noisy, sloppy, and in a hurry; fingers are sometimes clumsy and tasks need slowing down or repeated practice to achieve desired results

◆ May fall backward out of their chairs at this age rather than sideways as at five

◆ Children at this age are teething, so they often chew on pencils, fingernails, hair, books, and other objects

◆ Work in spurts and will tire easily; frequent illness and absence is not uncommon

◆ Enjoy being active, both inside and outdoors

◆ Good visual tracking from left to right and back to the beginning of the next line is normative as sixes begin to read

◆ Some will still have difficulty copying from board or chart; provide handouts for students to copy from at their desks

◆ When writing, find spacing and staying on the line difficult because they are more interested in process than product

◆ Often more comfortable standing up to work, even at their desks

SOCIAL AND EMOTIONAL DEVELOPMENT

◆ Ambitious; may choose projects that are too hard

◆ Proud of their accomplishments and highly competitive

◆ Sometimes "poor sports" or dishonest; may invent new rules so they can win; cooperative challenge activities take the edge off their fierce need to win individually

◆ Anxious to do well; extremely sensitive; severe criticism can truly be traumatic

◆ Tremendous capacity for enjoyment

◆ Can be bossy, teasing, or critical of others; bossy behavior is sometimes related to competition for friendships

◆ Tend to complain frequently and use tantrums, teasing, bossing, complaining, and reporting on classmates to try out relationships with authority; need adult understanding but also clear boundaries and limits for acceptable behavior; it can be helpful to read books about teasing, etc.

◆ Care a great deal about friends; may have a best friend

◆ Sometimes more influenced by happenings at school than at home

◆ Enjoy working and playing in groups; engage in more elaborate cooperative and dramatic play than at five

◆ Like doing things for themselves; ready to try taking on individual and group responsibility

COMMUNICATION, LANGUAGE, LITERACY

- Enjoy explaining things and sharing about things they like; partner sharing can serve as a helpful rehearsal before sharing with the class

- Use boisterous and enthusiastic language

- Love jokes and guessing games that the whole class can engage in; a fun activity is trying to guess a number by asking questions and explaining how they "got" the number before saying the answer

---

COGNITIVE CAPACITY

- Very curious; love discovery, new ideas, and asking questions

- Better understanding of past and present, long ago and far away; can begin to understand real history markers

- Very motivated to learn; enjoy the process more than the product; beginning to value skill and technique for their own sake

- Love to color, paint, read, and write; experience an artistic explosion; learn the most when teachers value their efforts and encourage risk-taking

- Comfortable with a busy level of noise and activity

- Enjoy and learn from games, poems, riddles, and songs

Sixes enjoy explaining what they know.

- ◆ Proudly produce a great quantity of work but are unconcerned with quality; can produce products of higher quality when encouraged to work more slowly or when teachers limit number or complexity of tasks

- ◆ Enjoy and learn from field trips followed by opportunities to tell about trips or use blocks to recreate things they saw

READING

Provide opportunities for children this age to:

◆ Continue partner reading

◆ Continue phonics learning through guided reading with the whole class and in small groups

◆ Continue reading predictable books while beginning to move on to easy chapter books

◆ Use writing, drawing, clay, painting, drama, or blocks to show their thoughts and feelings about a story

◆ Show their understanding of differences between genres (for example, poetry versus a report; fiction versus nonfiction)

WRITING

Expect from these children:

◆ **Writing** Story development still strongly influenced by drawings, for example, stories based on a collection of drawings; writing whole sentences that are early phonemic or use "letter name" spelling strategies—"I WNT TO HR HS" for "I went to her house"

◆ **Beginning spelling** Letter naming and "transitional" spelling ("My frends ride bickes"); emerging sense of phonetic clues

- **Writing themes** Best friends, school-related stories, family, pets, going on trips, new possessions, holidays, fantasy

- **Handwriting** Proper grasp of pencil; letters the same size or slightly larger than at five and more sloppily written because children are rushing or experimenting with new letter formation; spontaneous mixing of uppercase and lowercase letters; unpredictable spacing

---

MATH

Provide opportunities for children this age to:

- Do mental mathematics and written problem-solving after they've mastered the necessary skills with concrete materials

- Do basic computation with money, sometimes using a calculator or computer

- Complete simple worksheets, both paper and online, to practice basic computation (for example, "Mad Math Minutes" to check speed and accuracy of basic addition and subtraction)

- Experiment with reversing operations (+ and –)

- Do lots of measuring using sand or water tables, their feet, and blocks

- Work with manipulatives such as magnets, pulleys, puzzles, interlocking cubes, scoops, funnels, measuring cups, and sand

ACROSS THE CURRICULUM
(including social studies, languages, science, special areas)

Provide opportunities for children this age to:

◆ Take short "wiggle breaks" throughout the day

◆ Have a range of choices with different degrees of difficulty for working on classroom projects and representing learning

◆ Enjoy surprises and treats, including learning new games, inventing new characters, drawing treasure maps

◆ Use new tools such as magnifying glasses or field journals to draw in

◆ Make and use maps of the classroom, their room at home, or their route from home to school

◆ Practice newly learned techniques; for example, to help them understand how scientists observe and measure growth over time, they might draw pictures of a seed they plant in the classroom and draw its growth each day

◆ Experiment with clay, paints, dancing, coloring, book making, weaving, singing, and other arts

Sixes are eager to experiment with new art materials.

*Seven-year-olds are serious children who experience
the world with sensitivity.*

Seven-Year-Olds

"On a bicycle I traveled over the known world's edge, and the ground held. I was seven."

An American Childhood ✳ by Annie Dillard

I've noticed that seven-year-olds love to explore. We did a unit on insects, beginning with crickets. The children were really curious about the crickets, really wanted to look carefully at them. The students can also get attached. When we studied butterflies they didn't want to release them because a bird might get them.

—*Ramona McCullough*
Responsive Classroom Consulting Teacher,
Center for Responsive Schools

Seven-year-olds are serious children who see and feel with thoughtful intensity. After the outwardly expressive exuberance of six, sevens turn inward to consolidate the enormous cognitive and emotional growth they've just experienced. They become quieter and more sensitive, self-conscious, and self-absorbed as they figure out how to manage new feelings and cognitive structures. Seven is a year of moving forward cautiously, of craving security and structure while avoiding risk and uncertainty.

At home, sevens seek to spend a good deal of time alone, constructing their inward imaginings as they read, listen to music, or play with animals or dolls. At school, too, they appreciate quiet corners for reading or working. They like to work alone but also do well with partner work assigned by their teacher, with whom they appreciate having a personal relationship. They also enjoy focusing intensely on a relationship with one "best friend," although the best friend may change frequently.

Doing things with just-right precision matters very much to sevens. Whereas sixes are fond of the pencil sharpener, sevens adore the eraser. Concerned about both process and product, they want their work to be correct as well as beautiful and will labor long and hard to make it so. As they concentrate on getting every detail correct, seven-year-olds tend to miniaturize their writing, constructions, and elaborate, detailed drawings.

They're industriously creating tiny, intricate worlds that they try hard to control and perfect.

To get a feeling for seven-year-olds' skill at combining imagination and precision, picture a diorama that fits easily in a shoebox, complete with buildings, vehicles, trees, animals, and people smaller than clothespins, cut out of cardboard and adorned with colorful costumes. It's wonderfully illuminating to ask a seven-year-old about such creative work, whether art, a classroom project, or a fanciful invention at home. They'll speak with specificity and inevitably tell you about important details you've missed.

7-Year-Olds at Home

- Crave stability and predictability; you can help them feel safe and cared for by providing consistent schedules and routines

- Are often perfectionists and worry a lot about assignments and tests; you can help by listening to their concerns and offering support

- Often have a best friend, but who that friend is might change frequently

- Enjoy having chapter books read to them

- Can have quickly changing moods; close communication between school and home helps ensure children's needs are understood

At this age, children are driven by curiosity and a strong internal desire to discover and invent. They're intensely interested in how things work and love to take things apart and put them back together. They have a beginning understanding of the concepts of time and quantity and can increasingly represent their understandings symbolically through writing or drawing. Science and social studies take on new meaning as sevens become more interested in the world around them, and their increasing ability to infer, predict, and estimate makes second grade an ideal time to learn math concepts.

Sevens appreciate the beauty and wonder of the world and love using hand lenses and magnifying boxes to better discern the orderly arrangements of nature. They likewise love to have order around them and will generally keep their desks or table spots just so. With their penchant for orderliness, sevens enjoy tasks such as cleaning up, preparing snack, setting a table, and organizing blocks.

The overall structure and routine of school further support sevens' need for orderliness. In the classroom, they like to know what's coming next and to have time to get ready for each task, in which they can become completely absorbed. Time, in fact, matters very much to seven-year-olds. To feel comfortable and personally satisfied with their work, they need to finish what they're doing, saying, or thinking in a calm and unhurried way.

When we provide the predictability, security, structure, and time that sevens need and help them move forward in small

Sevens appreciate quiet spaces for working.

steps, these hard workers and positive perfectionists can accomplish so much. They adore parents and teachers who organize home and classroom in ways that honor this essential nature of being seven.

Typical Growth Patterns of 7-Year-Olds

PHYSICAL DEVELOPMENT

◆ Like confined spaces

◆ Improved coordination for both gross and fine motor skills

◆ More coordinated with throwing, catching, and other sports-related skills than at younger ages

◆ Muscles sometimes are tense; often hold pencil near the point with three-fingered, pincer-like grasp that they find difficult to relax

◆ Anchor their printing and drawing to the baseline; find filling up the line space difficult

◆ Increased ability to focus on objects nearby; often focus on a small, close area; writing, drawing, and numbers are tidy and small, if not microscopic

◆ Work with head down on desk, often covering or closing one eye

◆ Can be sensitive to many physical and psychosomatic hurts

◆ Often prefer video or online games to gym games, though still enjoy imaginary adventures outdoors

SOCIAL AND EMOTIONAL DEVELOPMENT

◆ Inward-looking; sensitive to others' feelings; empathetic

◆ Often have a best friend, although their best friend might frequently change

◆ Prefer working and playing alone or with one friend; enjoy one-on-one conversations and like to send notes

◆ Changeable; sometimes moody or pouty; may worry that "Nobody likes me!"

◆ Need security, structure, and stability; can be upset by changes in room arrangement or scheduling

◆ Will rely on adults for help and constant reassurance

◆ Extremely loyal to the classroom teacher; need teachers to prepare them in advance for substitutes

◆ Conscientious and serious about their schoolwork for the most part; don't like taking risks or making mistakes; can get sick from worrying about tests, assignments, etc.

◆ Have strong likes and dislikes

◆ Demonstrate desire to keep things neat and tidy

◆ Playground games such as jump rope, four square, and hop-scotch are more popular than team or large-group activities, although imaginary play remains strong

◆ Have a strong sense of right and wrong, and concern for others leads them to sometimes tell adults about classmates' behaviors

COMMUNICATION, LANGUAGE, LITERACY

◆ Listen well and speak precisely

◆ Rapidly develop their vocabularies; sevens love to keep notebooks of their new words

◆ Show great interest in meanings of words

◆ Secret codes, Morse code, and pig Latin can engage children at this age

---

COGNITIVE CAPACITY

◆ Like to repeat tasks; like to review learning verbally or frequently touch base in other ways with their teacher

◆ Weekly spelling and vocabulary lists and short tests are enjoyable for most students

◆ Like to work slowly and finish what they start; appreciate a "heads-up" that it's time to prepare for transitions; may find timed tests especially troublesome

◆ Bothered by mistakes and try hard to make their work perfect

◆ Enjoy inquiry activities and hands-on exploration; often work well in "discovery" centers

◆ Like to collect, sort, and classify

◆ Still like to be read chapter books by teachers and parents

◆ Enjoy board games as well as computer games; especially enjoy playing games with one other person

Seven-year-olds take time with their work and strive for accuracy.

- Increasingly able to share what they are learning and how they feel about it through verbal, written, and artistic reflections

- Need support for sustained, quiet work periods

- Enjoy memorization of poems, songs, chants, and cheers

- Comfortable with emphasis on high-quality products and proper display of work; able to accept feedback and revise work

- A few students still not fully able to read without vocalizing; still sometimes whisper to themselves during "silent" reading

READING

Provide opportunities for children this age to:

◆ Have time for individual reading (their greater strength at this age)

◆ Continue phonics work; children thrive on intense phonics instruction in small groups

◆ Do written reading comprehension assignments that are short and pithy; better to have students complete two or three questions thoughtfully than answer many test-like comprehension practice sheets

---

WRITING

Expect from these children:

◆ **Writing** Longer stories with a beginning, middle, and end, including "chapter" books in some cases; great interest in the story line; tendency to include lots of detail; writing before drawing and sometimes even writing without drawing; readiness to begin nonfiction writing as a way to show learning from science or social studies investigations

- **Spelling** Correct spelling slowly emerging from transitional spelling; increased phonetic and sight word fluency; ease in learning capitalization and punctuation; readiness for formal spelling program

- **Writing themes** Family and friends; sleeping over; losing teeth; trips; pets (often including stories about the death of a pet); nightmares; worries about the death of family members, illness, war, famine, or other serious issues

- **Handwriting** Letters are often microscopic in size

MATH

Provide opportunities for children this age to:

- Do more concrete manipulation and computation with money and time

- Do more complex mental mathematics and solve simple word problems using addition and subtraction

- Work with fractions by using rulers and scales to compare lengths and widths

- Experiment with symmetry and other simple geometry, such as by using unit blocks or pattern blocks

- Do simple computation with multiplication; do hands-on division with concrete materials such as counting cubes or plastic pizza pieces

- Continue practicing mathematical skills by playing games requiring counting and estimating to move board pieces (Parcheesi, Sorry, etc.)

ACROSS THE CURRICULUM
(including social studies, languages, science, special areas)

Provide opportunities for children this age to:

- Use programs such as PowerPoint to show what they've learned

- With support, take photos to incorporate into reports or class books

- Have choices in how they represent learning

- Take things apart and discover how they work; sort and classify things like buttons, pictures, leaves, shapes

- Expand vocabulary in all subject areas

- Play games and tell jokes as a way to moderate their seriousness

- Work with one partner rather than groups

Note the detail in this seven-year-old's watercolor: the wood grain, the deeper blue at the bottom of the vase, the changing background.

Eight-year-olds are full of energy and enthusiasm for new things.

Eight-Year-Olds

"Mothers for miles around worried about Zuckerman's swing. They feared some child would fall off. But no child ever did. Children almost always hang onto things tighter than their parents think they will."

Charlotte's Web ✳ by E. B. White

"Teacher, we have a great idea!" Watch out! Here come the eight-year-olds—full of energy, imagination, and little sense of their own limits.

"We have this great idea to do a play about Rosa Parks and we have all the clothes at home and we're going to bring them in tomorrow and we can use your desk for the bus and we can make tickets and charge admission and we'll put it on tomorrow . . . OK?"

There's no thought of a script, assigning parts, rehearsal schedules, or learning lines. It's all a blur of enthusiasm tempered by only a vague understanding of how things get done.

—*Chip Wood*

Eight-year-olds wake up in the morning with plans for adventure percolating before their feet hit the floor. To be eight is to be inventive and creative, full of energy, curiosity, and imagination, always in a hurry to try the next new thing—or to create the next new thing themselves. With a friend, or better yet, a group of friends, eights roll along with plans for a parade or a play, thrilled with their truly wonderful ideas for the "what" and blithely unconcerned with the "how."

Driven by their growing confidence and competence, eights eagerly learn the tools of their trade, whether pencil, pen, and ruler or computer, tablet, and app. They'll work hard at sketching and drawing, handcrafts, computer skills, and simple geometry, and they'll tackle school assignments with industrious verve, going for volume and speed over detail and accuracy. Social studies and science projects feed eight-year-olds' growing awareness of the wider world. Field trips to museums or outdoor spaces suit them beautifully by providing not only new experiences, but also lots of exploring and moving around with classmates and clipboards.

For all their excitement and industriousness, though, impatient eights are likely to become frustrated if accomplishments don't come easily or quickly; "I'm bored" usually means "This is too hard." To keep eights motivated and engaged, teachers can encourage them to keep trying, redirect their efforts when necessary so that they'll be more successful, and liberally display draft work along with finished, polished pieces.

Talkative, social eights enjoy and will happily share virtually any kind of humor, from riddles to rhymes to knock-knock jokes. They're typically ready to make new friends and seek out new adventures during a week away from home at overnight camp or whole days at a town or city recreation program. Whether at home or school, eights work and play well in groups.

As eight-year-olds tumble from one interest to another, exploring their world and their own potential, they excitedly keep track of the math facts they've memorized, the number of books they've read, how fast they can run, or how many limericks, dance steps, or soccer moves they've learned. They love to compare and compete, especially on sports teams and in classroom activities.

At no age do children benefit more from positive surprises than at eight. A small change of pace, such as pizza for breakfast or an unannounced afternoon visit to the school playground, will light up their day. Likewise, these novelty-loving children do best with chores at home and jobs at school when adults introduce a new roster of assignments before children tire of the old ones.

Such surprises and change-ups represent the sort of adult sensitivity that matters so much to eights. They need parents' and teachers' appreciation of their exploratory excitement, patience with their changeability, and gentle harnessing of their energy to give it direction and focus. Such adult responsiveness is key to supporting children during their busy and adventurous eighth year.

The expansive horizon is the vantage point of the eight-year-old who seeks new adventures, discoveries, and knowledge.

8-Year-Olds at Home

◆ Have lots of energy and a need for physical release; they play hard and tire quickly

◆ Love to tell jokes and share humor

◆ Have a growing moral sense and interest in fairness; you might hear cries of "It's not fair!"

◆ Might have a hard time remembering directions and homework assignments—help them establish a system or remind them to call an established "directions partner"

Typical Growth Patterns of 8-Year-Olds

PHYSICAL DEVELOPMENT

◆ Restless, full of energy, and often in a hurry; need physical release through outdoor play, and love group playground games such as Capture the Flag or Freeze Tag

◆ Play hard and tire quickly; do better with several short play breaks vs. one long break

◆ Growth spurts lead to some awkwardness in coordination

◆ Eyes focus well on objects near and far

◆ Better control of hands; can learn and use cursive writing if it is being taught

◆ Many using adult pencil grasp; some still need a pencil grip

SOCIAL AND EMOTIONAL DEVELOPMENT

◆ Like to socialize, often in the midst of individual or group work

◆ Love to share humor ("Have you heard the one about . . . ?")

◆ Love group activities and cooperative work; work best in groups that teachers change frequently throughout the year

- Adjust well to change; bounce back quickly from mistakes or disappointments

- May prefer working and playing with some classmates more than others; teacher leadership in whole-class games helps children mix

- Want peers' approval as much as the teacher's

- Respond well to class activities that build a sense of unity and cohesion, such as an annual spring hike or a service project to beautify the school

- Growing sense of moral responsibility and awareness of fairness issues beyond themselves; as a group, can rally around an issue that doesn't feel fair

- Form larger friendship groups than at seven

COMMUNICATION, LANGUAGE, LITERACY

- Vocabularies continue to expand rapidly

- Generally able to pay attention, but don't always remember what they've heard or are supposed to do; establishing "directions partners" can help them correctly record assignments and homework expectations and support each other outside of school if they forget homework directions

COGNITIVE CAPACITY

- Full of ideas; like to talk and explain ideas; tend to exaggerate

- Beginning to master handcrafts, computers, and drawing

- Very industrious; become engrossed in what they're doing, but have limited attention span; short exercise breaks help concentration

- Often take on more than they can handle; short assignments build confidence

- Enjoy responsibility, although do not always successfully complete tasks

- Usually organize work well; some need help with strategies like color coding their folders with stickers or putting due dates on assignments

- Show increasing interest in rules, logic, how things are put together, how things work, the natural world, and classification

- Can handle increasingly complex tasks but tire easily; may give up, but soon want to try again with a new idea about how to approach the task

- Care about both process and product of schoolwork, though they tend to be impatient and sloppy; love to add to work, but are not always interested in revising work

How Growth Patterns Relate to Learning

READING

Provide opportunities for children this age to:

- ◆ Work in groups reading trade books or in core reading programs keyed to their abilities and interests

- ◆ Begin reading independently and doing simple independent assignments, such as making book covers, conducting interviews, or building dioramas

- ◆ Do projects that spur interest in reading and research and allow them to be "experts" on a topic, and present what they've learned to the rest of the class

WRITING

Expect from these children:

- ◆ **Writing** Lengthy stories with increasingly descriptive language and much detail; interest in diverse kinds of writing, such as poetry, newspaper articles, and cartoons; beginning understanding of the importance of making drafts and revising

- ◆ **Spelling** Increasing ability to spell correctly; readiness to learn compound words, dictionary use, and alphabetical order; skill development to a level that makes lingering phonetic mistake patterns and real difficulty in spelling more obvious

CONTINUED ▶

◆ **Writing themes** Adventure, animals, sports with friends and heroes, unicorns and other mythical beasts, stories based on cartoons, poetry about nature and the seasons, nonfiction writing based on concrete science and social studies investigations

---

MATH

Provide opportunities for children this age to:

◆ Solve math problems using all four operations, as well as borrowing and carrying

◆ Study fractions by measuring, weighing, and doing more pencil-and-paper tasks to create graphs that demonstrate understanding of fractions in the real world

◆ Explore geometric patterns constructed with pencil and paper; manipulate geometric shapes on the computer

◆ Use geometric solids, math counters, rulers, balance scales, and other manipulatives to explain their thinking and problem-solving in concrete ways

◆ Use games as a way to practice and be able to explain math strategies (for example, predicting moves in checkers and chess or participating in whole-class guessing games, such as Guess the Number)

ACROSS THE CURRICULUM
(including social studies, languages, science, special areas)

Provide opportunities for children this age to:

- Use illustrations along with words to understand and analyze text

- Release physical energy through short activity breaks during the day and organized playground games at recess

- Work in cooperative groups, especially teacher-assigned groups that change frequently during the year

- Work on class projects that build unity, such as a service learning project

- Give each other support in remembering directions and assignments

- Develop their growing interest in how things work, classification, and the natural world through nonfiction reading in science and social studies

- Maintain a personal vocabulary notebook to record definitions of new words

Nine is an age of increasing self-definition.

Nine-Year-Olds

"My ninth year was certainly more exciting than any of the others. But not all of it was exactly what you would call fun."

Danny the Champion of the World ✳ by Roald Dahl

Sometimes the deep seriousness of nine-year-olds' social concerns brings a twinkle to the adult eye—as with the nine-year-old who worked diligently on her protest poster one Saturday morning: "Save the Elephants—Ban Ivory Soap."

—*Chip Wood*

There's an intense inner stirring in nine-year-olds as they become profoundly aware of the intricacies and subtleties of the world around them. This is a solemn age of intellectual stretching, wondering, arguing, questioning, and doubting—all signs of remarkable growth in these children's resilience, intellectual curiosity, maturing moral character, and capacity for independent thought.

During this year of realization and reflection, children impatiently question the ways adults have made the world—a world they begin to see they will have the power and responsibility to manage and to change. And what nines see is often the gloomy side of things. They worry about world events, moving away, parents' health, losing best friends, and changing schools, and they complain about aches and pains, cuts and bruises, and hurt feelings. They may twist their hair or bite their nails as they seek outlets for their physical and emotional tensions.

Fairness begins to matter a great deal as nines take on the cognitive task of understanding ethical behavior at a new level. They're concerned about global justice: Why are some people poor? Why are we allowing climate change to happen? Why are some people cruel to animals? Nines show concern about fairness on the local level, too, and often feel singled out for unfair treatment by a teacher, parent, or coach. Their complaints—signs of their increasing understanding of and sensitivity to how the world works—can also be a way for nines to express their growing sense of peer importance and group solidarity. They speak as one when they inform the grown-ups that "You're never fair to us!" or "We never get to do anything."

Nine-year-olds' peer solidarity can be channeled into wonderful club activities; they enjoy gathering to play chess or computer games or to share collections of rocks, stamps, book series, or the latest collectible cards or gadgets. They're likely, though, to be very competitive in these activities, as well as in the classroom and on the playground.

Nine is an age not only of growing peer identification but also of increasing self-definition. Each child's individual personality and way of presenting themselves to peers and meaningful adults stands out in clear relief. As they do this person-building work, nines can be very critical, both of themselves and of others. They

9-Year-Olds at Home

- ◆ Need your encouragement, listening, and understanding to balance their anxious approach to life
- ◆ Are trying out new ways of being, which often shows up as a new look—new hairstyle, new ways of dressing
- ◆ Are changeable, and moods and interests shift rapidly; this is a time to rent rather than buy musical instruments

need adults to recognize and validate their feelings of frustration and give them the tools to cope with those feelings.

Nines work with industrious care on appropriately challenging and purposeful school assignments and projects. They tend to learn better on their own as they master basic skills and gain a more solid understanding of key cognitive concepts such as multiplication, spelling patterns, and the scientific process. Students put a great deal of effort into final products and willingly study for the weekly spelling quiz or chapter test in math.

As these typically anxious children approach test-taking or other tasks they find challenging, they prefer caution to risk. By supporting nines with modeling, role-playing, and many opportunities for practice, teachers can help them stay calm and focused so they can make the best use of their growing intellectual capacities.

Adults' patient listening to and understanding of all their wonderings and worryings matter enormously to nine-year-olds. A sense of humor, a determined lightness, positive language and encouragement, "I like you just the way you are"—these gifts from teachers and parents help balance the weighty solemnity of nine and keep these brave explorers moving steadily forward into their ever-expanding universe.

Typical Growth Patterns of 9-Year-Olds

PHYSICAL DEVELOPMENT

◆ Better coordination is evident in most all physical activity

◆ Like to push their physical limits, but tire easily

◆ Restless; can't sit still for long

◆ With better fine motor coordination and control, show more interest in producing detailed drawings and illustrations, scientific notation, comic strips, and graphic novels

◆ Benefit from practice with a variety of fine motor tools and tasks (weaving, knitting, carving, drawing, etc.) to increase manual dexterity

◆ May twist hair, bite nails, or purse lips to relieve tension

---

SOCIAL AND EMOTIONAL DEVELOPMENT

◆ More individualistic; caught up in trying out new ways of dressing and grooming and trying on different personas

◆ Impatient and easily frustrated; often say "I hate it" or "It's boring" when work is difficult or repetitious; adult encouragement helps them persevere

◆ Often feel worried or anxious; complain of and sometimes exaggerate physical hurts; need adult lightheartedness and humor to relieve their anxiety and somberness

CONTINUED ▶

- Very critical of self and others (including adults); often complain about fairness issues

- Can be sullen, moody, aloof, and negative one minute and goofy and fun-loving the next

- Like to work with a partner of their choice

- Have a sense of who is in and who is out of certain groups in the lunchroom or on the playground; cliques may be problematic

- Very competitive; can work in groups but with lots of arguing

- Like to negotiate; this is the age of "Let's make a deal"

- Need adults to be patient and explain clearly, but concisely

---

COMMUNICATION, LANGUAGE, LITERACY

- Love descriptive language, word play, and new vocabulary; short dramatic skits or role-plays are popular

- Sometimes revert to baby talk when feeling anxious or silly

- Enjoy exaggeration, inappropriate jokes, and graffiti; adults need to be vigilant about how students are talking about marginalized people and what students are learning from the adults in their lives or online that reinforces stereotypes

- Enjoy and use technology and a range of social media to express ideas and thoughts

COGNITIVE CAPACITY

◆ Industrious and intellectually curious, but less imaginative than at eight; focus more on the "real" world; look hard (often anxiously) for explanations of facts, how things work, why things happen as they do

◆ Have trouble understanding abstractions, such as large numbers, long periods of time, or vast areas of space

◆ Beginning to be more aware, wondering about and exploring a bigger world of ideas, including issues of fairness and justice

◆ Able to manage more than one concept at a time (for example, when studying history, they can understand both "long ago" and "far away")

◆ Often ask, "Why do we have to do this?" and need homework related specifically to the next day's work

◆ Reading to learn instead of learning to read; most ready to read for information in books and newspapers and on websites

◆ Take pride in attention to detail and finished work, but may jump quickly between interests

◆ Able to copy from the board, recopy assignments, and produce visually attractive final drafts

How Growth Patterns Relate to Learning

READING

Provide opportunities for children this age to:

◆ Continue working in reading groups with focus on comprehension and interpretation

◆ Tackle assignments that involve beginning research tasks and use of related reading material

◆ Intensively develop dictionary skills introduced at earlier ages

◆ Volunteer to read orally during read-aloud

◆ Explore poetry seriously throughout the year as readers and writers

---

WRITING

Expect from these children:

◆ **Writing** Readiness for emphasis on first draft and revision process; ability to absorb teaching about descriptive writing, character development, plot, cohesiveness, and believability; frequent episodes of "writer's block"

◆ **Spelling** Improving use of dictionary; improving first-draft spelling; fewer mistakes with spelling in journals and subject writing; readiness for weekly spelling tests; mastery of basic capitalization and punctuation

◆ **Writing themes** Moving away, divorce, death, disease, and other worries; world issues; poetry about feelings and darker themes

---

MATH

Provide opportunities for children this age to:

◆ Practice division by measuring, working with fractions, doing surveys, graphing, and experimenting with standard algorithms

◆ Work extensively with word problems, including those of their own creation

◆ Compute with money and begin learning about decimals

◆ Practice multiplication tables (mastery at ten)

◆ Continue exploring math concepts with concrete objects and pictorial representations

ACROSS THE CURRICULUM
(including social studies, languages, science, special areas)

Provide opportunities for children this age to:

◆ Use and practice fine motor skills through printing, drawing, and crafts that require fine motor coordination

◆ Work with a partner of their choice some of the time; balance this with structures that help them work and play with all classmates, not just best friends

◆ Use drama to play with language and practice new vocabulary (for example, they could present a biographical sketch of a famous person and dress up in costume)

Nines make statements and share feelings, often dramatically and insistently, in their art, writing, and verbal opinions.

On Turning Ten

BY BILLY COLLINS

The whole idea of it makes me feel
like I'm coming down with something,
something worse than any stomach ache
or the headaches I get from reading in bad light—
a kind of measles of the spirit,
a mumps of the psyche,
a disfiguring chicken pox of the soul.

You tell me it is too early to be looking back,
but that is because you have forgotten
the perfect simplicity of being one
and the beautiful complexity introduced by two.
But I can lie on my bed and remember every digit.
At four I was an Arabian wizard.
I could make myself invisible
by drinking a glass of milk a certain way.
At seven I was a soldier, at nine a prince.

But now I am mostly at the window
watching the late afternoon light.
Back then it never fell so solemnly
against the side of my tree house,
and my bicycle never leaned against the garage
as it does today,
all the dark blue speed drained out of it.

This is the beginning of sadness, I say to myself,
as I walk through the universe in my sneakers.
It is time to say good-bye to my imaginary friends,
time to turn the first big number.

It seems only yesterday I used to believe
there was nothing under my skin but light.
If you cut me I would shine.
But now when I fall upon the sidewalks of life,
I skin my knees. I bleed.

"On Turning Ten" is from *The Art of Drowning* by Billy Collins,
©1995. Reprinted by permission of the University of
Pittsburgh Press.

Ten-year-olds love to work together and share ideas in groups.

Ten-Year-Olds

*"Mrs. Hanson told Diane and me to
get our folders and place them on our desks.
I made a pretty semicircle with mine. I was glad
I had only good papers for my parents to see."*

Nothing's Fair in Fifth Grade ✳ by Barthe DeClements

"Can we stay in today and finish the book?
Please!"

"Will you read more this afternoon, Mrs. Goodwin?
We promise to do our math for homework if you
would. This story is so awesome!"

"Yeah," comes the chorus of hushed voices.

"Well . . . all right, class . . . but just one more chapter," yields Mrs. Goodwin, silently delighting in one of those magic moments of teaching, one she will always treasure about this class.

The children settle back in, sprawling on the carpet, or chins on hands at their desks; two girls lean against Mrs. Goodwin as she reads from her comfy chair. The story continues.

Such scenes are repeated often when children are ten . . . the golden end of childhood.

—*Chip Wood*

Ten-year-olds can take on just about anything and delight in every minute of it. During this sunny year, children love to play, to learn, and to relate to others. This is a time for consolidating the gains from their early years as they find comfort in themselves, their teachers, their parents, and even their siblings. Tens relax in childhood as they gather strength for the impending challenges of adolescence.

Happy and easygoing tens generally look up to and admire their teachers and parents and take real pleasure in both family outings and teacher-led activities. They enjoy their classmates, too, and can engage productively in collaborative, project-based learning. Because of their relative calmness and instinct for getting along with others, ten-year-olds do well in a variety of group configurations, including mixed-age groups: They can often help elevens and even twelves in cooperative pursuits.

Ten is the ideal age for large-group efforts—think class trips, plays, and community service projects—as well as formal outdoor learning such as overnight camping or ropes courses. Ten-year-olds especially love outdoor group games and need physical play as much as younger children. They'll do equally well in noncompetitive activities and more traditional competitive games like kickball and tag. Boys and girls play well together in either type of activity or game.

At ten, children love learning factual information, and they're extraordinarily good at memorizing. These industrious children can solidify their multiplication tables easily; tackle spelling and vocabulary with relish; recite oodles of poems; take part in choral readings and songs; and memorize all the presidents, principal products of major nations, or lines of a play. And they delight in sharing their knowledge with classmates.

Given tens' capacity for retaining factual information, this is a good year for education about the human body, sex, and reproduction (as determined by the school's curriculum guidelines). Such teaching can be more effective now than in a year or two, when children are more self-conscious about their changing bodies.

With their receptive minds, ten-year-olds typically know all the rules. Given their sociability, they're likely to be in mutual agreement about how to follow those rules so they can get on with the fun of the game. The ten-year-old's agreeable acceptance of rules about how things work makes this a wonderful age for teaching or reteaching mediation and problem-solving and introducing governmental structures and scientific principles.

Ordering their world is central to ten-year-olds. Great organizers with a strong interest in classification and seriation, they relish their collections of baseball and superhero cards, rocks, coins, arrowheads, and animal figures. In their learning, they eagerly absorb the details of phylum and genus and other ways of classifying and ordering the world. Tens are also ready to take on real responsibility for keeping their school and home spaces neat and orderly.

Tens work hard at producing tangible products that display their competence—book reports, essays, beginning research writing, and scientific documentation. Now is the time when the study of music, dance, or sport becomes something they want to stick with and grow in.

Now is also a time when children respond particularly well to parents and teachers noticing and appreciating their contributions to classroom, school, friends, and family. Such positive adult recognition buoys the efforts and amplifies the joy of these busy, enthusiastic children.

10-Year-Olds at Home

- Love to read and should be encouraged to spend as much time on independent reading as they do on other home-work

- Enjoy spending time with family and peers and respond well to appreciation of their contributions and efforts

- Are solidifying likes and dislikes; this is a good age for committing to learning an instrument or sport

- Love order and are great at organizing things; this is the time for them to take increased responsibility for keeping their living space neat and organized

Typical Growth Patterns of 10-Year-Olds

PHYSICAL DEVELOPMENT

◆ Large muscles for jumping, running, and other big movements are developing quickly, although upper body strength is usually undeveloped

◆ Need a great deal of outdoor time with physical activity and challenge for large muscles; without adequate exercise, energy may spill over into acting out in the classroom

◆ Often write more sloppily than at nine because they are in a hurry

◆ As control of small muscles improves, they continue to enjoy precision tasks such as tracing, copying, making maps, and drawing cartoons

◆ Ready to start using tools such as compasses, protractors, rulers, and templates

◆ Frequent snacks and rest periods benefit rapidly growing bodies

SOCIAL AND EMOTIONAL DEVELOPMENT

◆ Generally happy and friendly; enjoy family, peers, and teachers

◆ Quick to anger and to forgive

- Usually truthful; developing more mature sense of right and wrong; able to learn peer mediation or problem-solving

- Highly sensitive to and able to resolve friendship and fairness issues

- Basically cooperative and flexible; do well with group activities and games, collaborative learning, and building a sense of whole-class cohesion

- Benefit from class problem-solving meetings, committee work to plan a field trip, and conducting school surveys

- Eager to reach out to others, such as through community service or tutoring younger children

- Appreciate being noticed and rewarded for their efforts

COMMUNICATION, LANGUAGE, LITERACY

- Listen well; enjoy talking and explaining, and can appreciate others' perspectives

- Read voraciously; important that their daily schedule have as much time for independent reading as for homework

COGNITIVE CAPACITY

- Very good at memorizing poetry, songs, times tables, geography, and mathematical steps and formulas

- Increasingly able to think abstractly

- Take great pleasure in collecting, classifying, and organizing

- Can concentrate for long periods

- Take pride in schoolwork; pay close attention to form, structure, directions, and organization

- Usually conscientious with homework

- Very eager to learn

- Enjoy rules and logic; good at solving problems

- Can pay attention to spelling, dictation, and penmanship simultaneously, but work may be somewhat sloppy as they learn to integrate these skills

- Enjoy choral reading, singing, poetry, and plays

How Growth Patterns Relate to Learning

READING

Provide opportunities for children this age to:

- Read, memorize, and recite poetry, do choral readings, and put on plays

- Read trade books centered on themes

- Read independently and indulge their desire to devour one book after another; read more and do fewer book projects

- Enjoy comic books and appropriate graphic novels

WRITING

Expect from these children:

- **Writing** Readiness to write lengthy stories, longer poems, first research papers, pieces about famous people—all usually filled with light and descriptive language; more frequent use of humor; more use of dialogue; realistic description of inter-action between characters

- **Spelling** Memorizing the spelling of difficult words, and using the words, properly spelled, in day-to-day writing

- **Writing themes** Friends, friends, and more friends in many adventures; time travel; letters to request information; notes to friends; reports

MATH

Provide opportunities for children this age to:

◆ Master multiplication tables

◆ Work extensively with decimals

◆ Compute extensively with fractions

◆ Use maps to measure and compute

◆ Do double-digit division

◆ Solve word problems, including those of their own creation

ACROSS THE CURRICULUM
(including social studies, languages, science, special areas)

Provide opportunities for children this age to:

◆ Get plenty of exercise

◆ Do precision tasks, such as drawing maps and using protractors

◆ Take part in clubs, activities, group games, and team sports

◆ Participate in class problem-solving meetings and take part in planning for whole-class events

◆ Reach out to others in the community through service projects or assisting younger grades

◆ Memorize, classify, organize, and solve logic problems

Ten-year-olds' artwork confidently represents their learning about the world they inhabit.

Eleven-year-olds love to debate and negotiate.

Eleven-Year-Olds

*"But let's face it: Understanding me—I mean
really understanding me and my nutty life—
isn't so easy. That's why it's so hard for me to find
people I can trust. . . . So mostly I don't trust
anybody. Except my mom, Jules.
(Most of the time, anyway.)"*

Middle School: The Worst Years of My Life

✳

by James Patterson and Chris Tebbetts

It's near the end of the morning's math lesson.
The children are growing fidgety, but the teacher
presses on.

"What's another name for a parallelogram? . . . Yes, Max?"

"It's past time for recess. We're missing our recess!"

A chorus of agreement greets the teacher.

Finally out at recess, the fifth and sixth graders mill around on the kickball field.

"Same teams as yesterday!" yells one girl.

"No way!" screams another. "You smushed us yesterday."

"Yeah, but Jamal isn't here today, so that makes it even," says the first girl.

"Yeah, but look who you got today," says the other.

 The arguments continue. They use up ten full minutes of their precious recess time making up teams. No one seems to mind.

—*Chip Wood*

Elevens are, in a sense, electrified. As adolescence begins, cognitive structures in the brain are rewiring themselves at the same amazing speed with which the body is beginning to transform. Relationships with peers and adults are turning topsy-turvy. At home and in school, academically and socially, eleven-year-olds are busy engaging whole new worlds with a sense of outward boldness, yet inward tentativeness. Their lives crackle with the energy of change as they begin to establish a sense of physical and emotional identity.

Both girls and boys grow increasingly self-conscious about their changing bodies. Some boys grow rapidly taller; many struggle with clumsiness in athletics (as well as at twelve and thirteen). Many girls also experience a physical growth spurt, begin menstruating, and become more emotionally sensitive and volatile. Changing bodies affect some girls' willingness to continue in individual activities such as dance, gymnastics, or swimming. For both boys and girls, bones tend to grow faster than muscles, and complaints about aches and pains are common.

This is a year when students become much more devoted to their classmates and peer groups. With their growing interest in peers, elevens do well with collaborative work. They're likely, though, to challenge, debate, and argue with each other as they practice the art of social negotiation, which will help them form strong affiliations and friendships as teenagers and young adults.

Cliques—common among girls at this age—offer further practice in social negotiations. It's important, of course, for adults to step in if elevens' nascent skills at forming bonds inadvertently lead to bullying.

Eleven-year-olds generally love being physically active outdoors but often spend a good deal of time arguing about team effort and the interpretation of rules. Elevens often focus on their own personal skill development in a sport and constantly compare themselves with the best athletes. Some will drop out of competitive sports around this age as competition gets increasingly serious and the skills more difficult. Teachers and coaches can encourage participation by focusing on effort rather than perfection—by recognizing students who try hard as well as those who score.

Elevens also do well with projects and service learning, especially when their ideas are incorporated into the assignments. Tackling new and demanding skills in research, such as footnoting, finding and assessing online sources, creating bibliographies, and using scientific notation, feeds elevens' increasing cognitive strengths. So does exploring brand-new areas of knowledge, such as foreign languages, music, and forms of artistic expression. Elevens would rather learn new skills than hone old ones, yet revision and final-draft excellence in their schoolwork is a source of pride. Still, they tend to be easily frustrated and to voice that frustration in complaints, even as they continue to relish the challenges of their new learning.

Besides learning new school skills, eleven-year-olds also thrive on opportunities to learn life skills in the real world. They might interview the fire chief, take notes at a town meeting, or write letters to a corporation or an international humanitarian or environmental organization about an issue that concerns them. And they can do these and other assignments with a good measure of responsibility and independence.

11-Year-Olds at Home

- Stay up late and have trouble getting up in the morning; one way to ensure adequate sleep is to set limits on use of electronic devices

- Might have more behavior problems at home than they do at school, and you might hear from teachers about positive contributions in school even though this doesn't match what you see at home; it's important to continue setting clear limits and remember not to take things personally— your empathy and sense of humor will help elevens cope with their rapid physical and emotional changes

- Might have a hard time managing time and getting homework done, but it's helpful to leave homework consequences in the school's hands; check in with your child and with teachers, but don't try to manage too closely, as this is an important developmental struggle for adolescents as they learn to take independent responsibility for work

Strong believers and powerful advocates, eleven-year-olds speak passionately about their ideas, opinions, and allegiances. They also challenge adult judgments they once accepted. Indeed, these students are busy questioning and challenging all of their assumptions about the world, often awkwardly and sometimes in ways that may seem off target or downright rude. Yet elevens are often surprised that adults take offense at their challenges, and they are easily hurt and very uncomfortable when corrected in front of classmates. It's important to remember that their challenges and apparent disrespect are signs of their immense cognitive and social-emotional growth, of awakening powers that they do not yet know how to handle.

Along with challenging adults on nearly every topic, students at this age will likely respond to adult questions and directives with eye rolling, deep sighing, shrugging, and other postures that may seem contemptuous. Yet these responses are just outward signs that the eleven-year-old is practicing distancing—a way to establish physical and social safety when feeling uncomfortable or threatened. This distancing is an essential part of growing up, and who better to practice with than trusted teachers or parents?

In fact, elevens very much need solid connections to trusted adults who can see through their seemingly rude behavior and realize that feelings and relationships are seldom clear or simple for them. "Communication at a distance"—teachers responding in writing to students' journal entries, parents leaving a note at the bedside—enables adults to respect elevens' need for independence while continuing to build strong relationships with them.

*Eleven-year-olds love to explore different perspectives;
their work is often complex and invites conversation.*

This adult balancing act of staying close but not too close rec-
ognizes and honors the very "in between" nature of students in
their eleventh year. They're ready to spread their wings and take
short flights from the nest, but they're often less sure of themselves than they sound, sensitive and easily embarrassed as they
take their first clumsy but momentous steps toward establishing
independence and identity—the chief task of adolescence.

Typical Growth Patterns of 11-Year-Olds

PHYSICAL DEVELOPMENT

- Restless and very energetic

- Need lots of food and physical activity, and much more sleep than they usually get

- Girls may experience an early adolescent growth spurt and sexual maturation; some boys begin rapidly growing taller

- Although many still struggle with clumsiness, motor skills (such as throwing, catching, and kicking) begin to improve; like to measure their individual best

---

SOCIAL AND EMOTIONAL DEVELOPMENT

- Need reasonable amount of time to talk with peers; heavy users of social media

- Can seem impulsive; often talk before thinking

- Often behave best when away from home

- Need adult empathy, humor, and sensitivity to help them cope with their maturing minds and bodies

- Desire to test limits and rules is an important developmental milestone, not a personal attack on a teacher or parent

- Love the challenge of competition; prefer team sports and getting better at playing as a team

- Inclusion/exclusion issues loom large; worry more about who's "in" and who's "out" than when they were younger; may be cruel, sometimes physically aggressive

- Are sometimes moody, self-absorbed, and sensitive

COGNITIVE CAPACITY

- Would rather learn new skills than review or improve previous work

- Have trouble making decisions and are defensive about mistakes

- Becoming more adept at abstract thinking and deductive reasoning

- Enjoy the challenge of reasonably hard work

ETHICS AND SELF-DIRECTION

- Increasingly able to see the world from different points of view and perspectives of other cultures

- Like to challenge rules, argue, and test limits

- Class meetings, peer mediation, and cross-age tutoring can be highly effective in resolving issues

Class meetings are an effective way for eleven-year-olds to resolve issues.

MOVING TOWARD INDEPENDENCE

◆ Enjoy arguing and debating; appreciate humor

◆ Imitate adult language

◆ Learn well in collaborative groups; changing the composition of these groups as needed can help adjust the social mix and address inclusion/exclusion concerns

◆ Self-absorbed and interested in imagining themselves in adult roles; this makes history, biography, and current events exciting

◆ May show interest in and facility for languages, music, or mechanics; need opportunities to explore these areas

◆ Interested in learning about older and very young people

◆ Enjoy challenging tasks, but might need help with time management and homework skills

How Growth Patterns Relate to Learning

READING

Provide opportunities for students this age to:

◆ Take on week-long reading assignments, still using trade books

◆ Do more nonfiction reading tied to subjects that interest them

◆ Read biographies and scientific history; build timelines

◆ Read to children in younger grades

WRITING

Expect from these students:

◆ **Writing** Willingness to practice, although revision can be a struggle; writing that incorporates personal interests and is more adult-like in plot, character development, and style; very rudimentary research reports; enjoy poetry writing, cartooning, and journaling

◆ **Spelling** Ease and accuracy for some, with most enjoying the challenge of spelling difficult words; readiness to learn more dictionary skills

◆ **Writing themes** For most, blood and gore, fantasy, science fiction, love and romance; for advanced writers, experimentation with a variety of personally compelling themes

MATH

Provide opportunities for students this age to:

- Solve complicated word problems

- Study probability and statistics through real-world problems; do data searches online and through newspapers and magazines

- Use calculators and computers as problem-solving tools

- Work on speed and accuracy in computations

- Work with percentages

ACROSS THE CURRICULUM
(including social studies, languages, science, special areas)

Provide opportunities for students this age to:

- Take quiet breaks during the day for needed physical rest, as well as a break from academics and intense social-emotional dynamics

- Argue and debate in a safe environment

- Undertake scientific study, mathematical problem-solving, and invention

- Engage in "adult" academic tasks such as conducting Internet research, interviewing, footnoting, and creating a bibliography

At eleven, competition can be both friendly and fierce.

◆ Establish and modify rules and develop hypotheses about cause and effect, propose and test alternative hypotheses, and use rubrics to evaluate their work

◆ Learn through activities such as board games, intellectual puzzles, and brain teasers

Twelve-year-olds invest deeply in purposeful schoolwork.

Twelve-Year-Olds

"I am not a nut. I am a pioneer."

The Real Me ✳ by Betty Miles

One day, I witnessed a group of students invite a new student who was sitting all alone to eat lunch with them. They asked this new student tons of questions and made an effort to get to know him. I was surprised because this was a group that often sat together and seldom invited others to join them. Their response: "It's lunch time, and no one should sit alone at lunch." It reminded me how critical empathy is at this age.

—Joe Tilley
Professional Development
Designer and Consultant,
Center for Responsive Schools

"Gregarious" is a word well suited to twelves. They move into their widening world with great energy, eager to grow academically and socially, to build solid relationships, to explore all they can do and be as they sense their adult personalities beginning to unfold. "Confusion" also describes what it's like to be twelve. On the cusp of adolescence, twelves can be changeable and unpredictable as they come to terms with rapidly growing bodies, sort out new feelings, and strive to forge more grown-up identities.

As the search for identity intensifies, twelves' greatest need is to be with their friends. They spend hours texting and talking, evaluating and comparing notes on clothes, shoes, hairstyles, sports teams, movies, books, and music. The complement to this excited sharing with peers is enormous amounts of time spent alone in front of the mirror as twelves reflect on who they are becoming.

Along with intense enjoyment of their peers, twelves generally enjoy talking with adults outside the home and can do so with friendliness and a sense of confidence. Yet, twelves can also be unpredictable and hard to read. One day, they fervently want to do schoolwork as part of a group; the next day, they just as fervently want to work alone. They often say "That's not what I meant!" when a teacher misreads their seemingly rude tone or comment. At home, moody, introverted, or childish behavior and one-word responses reflect their need to rest and regroup in a safe environment.

Twelves can become deeply invested in purposeful schoolwork. They're excited by lengthy homework assignments and projects that culminate in visible products: reports with beautiful illustrations, historical skits with elaborate costumes and props, 3D topographical maps, scientific models with working parts, complex computer programs. Research projects, current events, environmental issues, community service projects, scientific experiments, major art projects, and dramatic productions can invite and engage twelve-year-olds.

12-Year-Olds at Home

- Are clearly into an adolescent sleep pattern and might have difficulty getting up in time for school

- Care more about peers' opinions than those of the adults in their life

- Are increasingly able to organize thoughts and set realistic short-term goals

- Want parents to listen to their ideas, though it may not always appear so

- Need a range of trusted adults in their lives to listen and advise; you can seek out such trusted adults to be a part of your preteen's life

- Can take on jobs to earn money, such as mowing lawns, babysitting, or delivering newspapers

When offered reasonable responsibilities at school, most twelves respond with pride. In fact, the more responsibility they're given, the better they do academically and socially. With adult help, twelves can manage a school store or recycling program, collect goods for families in need, or put out a class newspaper. Twelves make excellent one-on-one tutors for younger children or helpers in preschool or kindergarten classes. Many show amazing leadership potential and thrive on their first forays into student government and peer mediation.

In an apparent paradox, twelves may be almost comically irresponsible with smaller and more mundane responsibilities, such as keeping personal spaces neat at home and keeping track of assignments, books, papers, and gym clothes at school. This is the age of excuses, often transparent and humorous: "The printer chewed up my paper," "My baby sister erased all my files," "I left my book on the bus," "You didn't tell us it was due today," and on and on, even including the oldest homework excuse in the world: "My dog ate it." For twelves, this seeming paradox in responsibility-taking is simply a matter of priorities. Adults can help with fair and firm rules and discussions of consequences for items lost and tasks left undone.

Adult firmness also helps twelves navigate their reasonable and unreasonable ideas for changing the way home and school operate. As their interest in fairness grows, they need opportunities to discuss and modify rules and routines, along with the structure provided by adult consistency and clear, calm authority.

Twelves make excellent one-on-one tutors for younger children or helpers in preschool or kindergarten classes.

Twelves find deep meaning in rituals and ceremonies that recognize their growth and can prepare for these events seriously, with a strong sense of purpose. Service and athletic awards, honor assemblies, family social or religious traditions—all such rites of passage give twelves tangible recognition that they are indeed ready to begin the transition into adolescence, with its promise of widening horizons, adult-like roles, and responsible participation in society.

Typical Growth Patterns of 12-Year-Olds

PHYSICAL DEVELOPMENT

◆ Very energetic; need lots of exercise to rejuvenate their oxygen-hungry brains, along with lots of sleep and food (including in-school snacks)

◆ Have growth spurts

◆ Stay up late and then want to sleep late; might have trouble getting to school on time

SOCIAL AND EMOTIONAL DEVELOPMENT

◆ Adult personality begins to emerge; may try on different personalities along the way

◆ Capable of self-awareness, insight, and empathy; more reasonable and tolerant than at eleven

◆ May make new friendships with classmates they have not been friends with before

◆ Enthusiastic and spontaneous; appear to feel secure

◆ Understand the idea of training and regular exercise as a means to improve physical ability, but don't always follow through with routines and practice

- Care more about peers' opinions than those of teachers and parents

- Can help peers significantly with schoolwork; will make good use of time allowed for peer conferencing and partner projects, especially where their choices of subject matter and work partners are honored

- More able to handle lengthy homework assignments spread over several days, though these can be problematic if they extend over weekends; weekly or monthly planners are useful at this age

COGNITIVE CAPACITY

- Increasingly able to plan, organize thoughts and work, and set short-term goals, and appreciate the need to do so; will take advice from teachers they trust

- More able to think abstractly about complex moral issues

- May begin to excel at a subject (such as science) or a skill (such as drawing)

- Can better integrate their learning when schools use cross-disciplinary teaching models where teachers work together on projects, modeling for students how to do this with their peers

ETHICS AND SELF-DIRECTION

◆ Able to see both sides of an argument, but still like to argue one point of view

◆ Find current events, civics, and history highly motivating when tied to issues of clear relevance to their lives; formal debate structures can be used to organize meaningful listening to different perspectives

◆ Appreciate teachers who listen and respond to their suggestions for changes in routines, when realistic

◆ Both playful and serious; love to play class games but can have a serious discussion a moment later

---

MOVING TOWARD INDEPENDENCE

◆ Understand and enjoy word play and more sophisticated jokes; like to try out new vocabulary

◆ Enjoy conversation with adults and peers, gaining confidence in their ideas and opinions

◆ Enjoy trying out the latest slang from music and pop culture

◆ Will initiate their own activities without adult prompting; like to invent games, and will pursue social action both in and out of school

◆ Leadership qualities abound; thrive on opportunities for activities such as cross-age tutoring, jobs at school, community service, hosting visitors, and providing child care during parent meetings

Twelves are increasingly able to combine accurate scientific observation with careful artistic composition.

◆ Need access to significant adults, other than teachers and parents, who will listen to them and help them think about serious issues such as drugs, alcohol, sex, violence, and family problems

◆ Want to make money from jobs at home or in their neighborhood, such as mowing lawns, babysitting, or delivering newspapers

READING

Provide opportunities for students this age to:

◆ Continue independent reading of trade books with varied choices of titles and of projects to represent what they have learned from their reading; favorite topics include history, sports, science fiction, and fiction with themes tied to current events and social justice

◆ Read newspapers and magazines for current events information, work with charts and graphs, and use books and other written sources for scientific information

◆ Read trilogies and book series, where they can watch characters and themes develop over time

◆ Recognize and discuss formal aspects of fiction, such as setting and character, in formal reading groups or book groups

◆ Complete research reports based on readings from several sources, citing evidence and discerning factual data from "fake" information

◆ Learn research skills, such as using an online library catalog, working with an atlas, doing computer searches

WRITING

Expect from these students:

◆ **Writing** Increased facility with revision, particularly when changes result from peer conferences; interest in writing biographies and autobiographies, brief essays about world concerns (such as racism, poverty, and environmental issues), and pieces linked to reading-program genres (such as diaries, fantasies, and myths); interest in working on school newspaper; enjoyment of student-led conversations about their writing

◆ **Spelling** Functional for most; spell checkers and other computer interventions useful for those needing additional help

◆ **Writing themes** Summarizing and writing briefly and clearly about adolescent issues (sex, drugs, music, cars); emotional poetry; "editorial" writing full of extreme positions (class newspapers are a popular outlet); use of vernacular or slang in fiction; interesting dialogue

MATH

Provide opportunities for students this age to:

◆ Begin pre-algebra studies through extensive work with unknowns

◆ Use math as a tool for understanding science through exploration of such things as estimating or calculating distance in astronomy or graphing climate change over time

CONTINUED ▶

- Compute extensively with decimals, fractions, and percents and represent and illustrate using all of these methods

- Solve simple geometric problems using equations and measurements, such as area of different sizes of circles or triangles

- Use calculators, computers, and apps

ACROSS THE CURRICULUM
(including social studies, languages, science, special areas)

Provide opportunities for students this age to:

- Work with partners in peer conferences and projects

- Have choices in what they do, how they do it, and whom they work with

- Pursue interests in civics, history, current events, politics, social justice, and environmental issues, as well as pop culture

- Take part in formal debates

- Take a leadership role and engage in a variety of service projects

- Increase their digital skills

Twelves enjoy illustrating their stories, creating comic strips, and writing poetry and song lyrics.

Thirteen-year-olds have their own particular points of view and also look to peers for what's "cool" today.

Thirteen-Year-Olds

"*Today I am a teenager. I don't know
what I'm feeling right now.*"

The Diary of Latoya Hunter: My First Year in Junior High

✳

by Latoya Hunter

"This assignment stinks," says Jason, sitting across the table from Phoebe.

"I know," says Phoebe, "I have so much to do. And they give you this science project to do, too!"

"I know, they give it all at once!" says Jason through clenched teeth.

"I have softball," mirrors Phoebe through her braces, getting into it, "every day during vacation!"

—*Chip Wood (overheard in seventh grade
language arts class)*

Thirteen is an age of dramatic contrasts. Because thirteen-year-olds commonly slip backward developmentally as well as move forward, they may seem like younger twelve-year-olds one day and more mature than they really are the next. They want adults to notice, listen, and talk to them but also to leave them alone. They're engaged one minute and bored the next, suddenly confident and just as suddenly unsure, alternately outgoing and withdrawn, brooding alone and then shrieking and shouting with friends. Luckily, thirteens' high energy, along with a keen sense of humor and silliness, balance moody sensitivity and help power these rapidly transforming adolescents through the whirlwind of their thirteenth year.

Looking at the world from new points of view is the job of the thirteen-year-old, and it's one they do with delight and bravado. Arguing is a sport and a leisure pastime, and thirteens are likely to challenge parents, teachers, and classmates alike as they work to solidify their personalities, understand how the world operates, and get that world to recognize them as important individuals.

Physically and emotionally, never is the difference between the sexes more noticeable than it is at thirteen. Excitement and concern about the significant physical changes of puberty—that sure sign of growing up—are common. But while most girls have begun menstruating and experiencing other physical changes associated with sexual maturity, sexual changes are just beginning for the boys, most of whom won't experience all these changes until fourteen or fifteen. Emotionally, girls are ready to focus on close friendships, whereas boys travel in small groups and still engage in the jokey goofing around of their younger years.

13-Year-Olds at Home

- Are experiencing a sometimes bumpy transition to increasing independence—maintain your sense of humor and empathy as you help them navigate this terrain

- Are often ready for more freedom balanced by more responsibility; for example, this is a good time to give teens more control over their own space—how it is decorated, who can enter, how things are organized—along with new responsibilities for maintaining the space

- Have a tendency to hibernate and isolate; to counter this, offer access to afterschool clubs, teams, art or music lessons, family gatherings or work parties, and camp or rec programs

- Often have strong opinions about teachers, both positive and negative; listen to concerns they bring up, but keep in mind that these judgments are extremely changeable and might not require adult intervention (sometimes, however, it becomes clear the student needs your help to navigate a particular class or teacher)

Despite such notable differences, both boys and girls at thirteen share excitement about possible new freedoms and informal rites of passage—having more control over time spent with digital devices; being in a school with higher grade levels, often with or near high school students; studying harder subjects; and going places with just their friends.

Friends, in fact, are critical to thirteens, who seek belonging and significance primarily from their peers. They spend a great deal of positive energy trying to fit in and need lots of unstructured (but monitored) group time. Yet, in a classic expression of the contrasts of thirteen, they also crave time by themselves and can be quite introspective, with a propensity to seclude themselves in their bedrooms or personal spaces.

It's important to help thirteens balance their hibernating tendencies with forays into the wider world. Parents can offer opportunities to participate in afterschool clubs, teams, art or music lessons, family gatherings or work parties, and camp or rec programs. Schools can encourage participation in sports, music ensembles, student governance, community service projects, and other structured activities. Such experiences help these adolescents develop the cognitive, social-emotional, and moral strength they'll need as adults.

Thirteen-year-olds generally succeed in balancing increased responsibility with the increased freedom they're asking for. Indeed, learning to manage this balance is essential for developing a healthy identity. At home, parents can offer these teens more control over their personal space—when parents get to enter, how the space is decorated and organized (or not organized)—while transferring some responsibility for care of the contents, such as laundry, to the proud owner. Parents can also offer a choice of meaningful jobs that require more skill—cooking a simple meal for the family, say, versus taking out the trash. At school, teachers can invite thirteens to participate in classroom governance, help plan a major field trip, or tutor younger children.

School can present challenges as well as exciting opportunities for this age. Students who complain that teachers are boring often mean that teachers are not giving them enough attention and acknowledging them as important individuals. Yet thirteens often protect their fragile sense of self by becoming withdrawn and sensitive at school, tentative and hesitant when faced with academic challenges. They need supportive teachers who observe closely, listen carefully, and gently encourage risk-taking in the classroom.

During this year of excitement and confusion, adventurousness and sensitivity, thirteens very much need adult encouragement and support—especially from parents and teachers who accept the inconsistencies of the age with both humor and respect, who understand that from the chaos of early adolescence, an increasingly independent and capable young person will soon emerge.

Typical Growth Patterns of 13-Year-Olds

PHYSICAL DEVELOPMENT

◆ Lots of physical energy

◆ Skin problems are common; hygiene becomes more important

◆ Most girls are menstruating and have reached almost full physical development

◆ Most boys are showing first signs of puberty (they will reach full development at fourteen or fifteen)

◆ Health and sex education classes, as well as PE (including dressing and showering), often embarrass them and lead to silly or rude behavior

SOCIAL AND EMOTIONAL DEVELOPMENT

◆ Pay close attention to peers, who mirror what's in and what's out

◆ Moody and sensitive; may shut down and withdraw, or suddenly flare up in anger

◆ Their feelings are easily hurt, and they can easily hurt others' feelings; frequent meanness may stem from being insecure or scared and from not wanting to be left out

◆ Girls tend to focus on close friendships or cliques; boys tend to travel in small groups

- Spend hours using social media or playing video games

- Feel and exert a lot of peer pressure concerning what to wear, how to talk, what music to listen to

- Most show a strong interest in sports

- Worry and complain about schoolwork and homework

- Increasingly punctuate their humor with sarcasm

- Often quieter and more secretive than twelves or fourteens

COGNITIVE CAPACITY

- Continued growth in abstract reasoning—making assumptions, developing hypotheses

- Tentative, worried, and unwilling to take risks on tough intellectual tasks

- Likes and dislikes become more pronounced; for example, may love math and hate English

- Think about many sides of an issue or solutions to a problem

ETHICS AND SELF-DIRECTION

- Like to challenge intellectual as well as social authority, often for the sake of argument

- Interested in issues of fairness and justice; want to serve others

CONTINUED ▶

◆ May need more support than twelves or older teens when working in groups; tend to argue or complain about fairness, and often prefer solitary activity or working with a single partner

◆ Highly judgmental of teachers, either positively or negatively; like to discuss opinions about teachers with other students and parents

◆ Can think globally, but often can't put ideals into practice in day-to-day life; for example, concerned about social justice issues, but often mean to each other

MOVING TOWARD INDEPENDENCE

◆ Some are very interested in and influenced by popular culture, while others march to the beat of their own drum

◆ Sometimes shut down and answer adults' questions with a single word, but might be just as likely to respond with loud, extreme language

◆ Very concerned about personal appearance, but unconcerned about the neatness of their personal environment, such as rooms at home or lockers and desks at school

◆ Benefit from opportunities to balance teacher evaluation and grading with self-evaluation of their schoolwork through the use of rubrics that they may help create (for example, in judging project-based learning assignments)

◆ Will challenge teachers by asking "Why do we have to learn this?" but will accept a calm and thoughtful response from the teacher

How Growth Patterns Relate to Learning

READING

Provide opportunities for students this age to:

◆ Read fiction and nonfiction involving social issues through assigned and leveled reading groups, sometimes with choice of titles

◆ Extensively study literary elements—plot, character, mood, setting, and theme—and talk meaningfully about these elements in class

◆ Read aloud to the class from articles they have found or the teacher provides; use sources dealing with social topics, such as conformity, crime, and homelessness, as springboards to discussion and deeper understanding

◆ Acquire vocabulary from context along with consulting a dictionary and thesaurus; a vocabulary "word of the day" can be popular

◆ Use textual references to document and defend their points of view

WRITING

Expect from these students:

- ◆ **Writing** Ability to revise with careful attention to the difference between critique and personal criticism; beginning ability to structure short expository essays with a thesis statement and supporting details; ability to summarize

- ◆ **Spelling** Functional for most (those with ongoing spelling difficulty appreciate spell checkers)

- ◆ **Writing themes** Topics in curricular literature; social peer issues that focus on justice versus injustice and inclusion versus exclusion

---

MATH

Provide opportunities for students this age to:

- ◆ Review all operations, with special emphasis on conversion of decimals, fractions, and percents, and use their increasingly facile ability to move from one operation to another to represent understanding numerically

- ◆ Make mathematical sets and do attribute mapping; study number patterns; explore Fibonacci, binary, geometric, and other number sequences

- ◆ Extensively use geometric tools, such as the compass and straightedge, in sophisticated ways to construct and organize space

- ◆ Develop an extensive geometric vocabulary

- Engage in mathematical conversations about the concept of zero and negative numbers

- Begin learning more sophisticated algebra than simple equations with one unknown

---

ACROSS THE CURRICULUM
(including social studies, languages, science, special areas)

Provide opportunities for students this age to:

- Have short, regular, predictable homework assignments directly related to the next day's assignments; check their homework in small groups at the beginning of the school day, which builds academic collaboration

- Choose partners or group members, but teachers need to monitor the tone and process of collaborative work and assign partners or groups if needed for safety

- Consider and debate many sides of an issue

- Develop skills of abstract thinking and safely take intellectual risks, such as thinking of a range of ways to solve a problem or multiple possibilities about what causes it

- Help create rubrics for self-evaluation of work

- Plan service projects like food drives or community cleanups

Truly listening to fourteen-year-olds is a powerful way to connect with them.

Fourteen-Year-Olds

"When there are many worlds
you can choose the one
you walk into each day."

Brown Girl Dreaming ✳ by Jacqueline Woodson

"This stuff always happens to me!" exclaims Gloria. "I want to be a teacher and on the survey it says I'm going to be a farmer. I like frogs and I have some at home," she jokes.

"I lived on a farm once," says another girl at her table.

"Remember when we made fences for the play?" interjects a third girl, ignoring the second girl's comment.

"Yeah, in fourth grade!" Gloria responds. "Doesn't your earring hurt?" she says, turning to face the second girl. "What happened to your face?"

"I got hit in softball with a line drive," she tells Gloria.

"Did it hurt?" Gloria asks, taking the rubber bands from her braces and popping a piece of gum in her mouth.

—*Chip Wood (overheard in a math class)*

To fourteen-year-olds, the question "Who am I?" seems best answered in terms of "Who are *we*?" The way that others see these students seems to matter more to them than how they see themselves. Fourteens are moving steadily toward peers and away from parents and teachers as the central figures in their lives. They bond in small social groups, travel street and school together, and pour enormous physical, emotional, and cognitive energy into developing an adolescent subculture. These are steps in the distancing dance of fourteen-year-olds, outward signs that they are doing the all-important inward work of their age: forging a stronger sense of both personal and group identity.

Less mercurial than at thirteen, funny, creative, highly energetic, and often very loud, fourteens think and reason more abstractly than they did at thirteen and have a more adult-like sense of right and wrong. Despite their preoccupation with what others think of them, they show definite growth in their ability to self-evaluate, to be more aware of their own gifts and challenges.

Fourteens also communicate more easily with other teens than they did just a year ago and delight in being on board with their peer group's music, language, clothes, hairstyles, likes, and dislikes. These portable image advertisements serve the critical functions of attracting other teens while simultaneously tending to put off adults. Fourteens' interest in peers extends quite definitely to sexual awareness. Boys are becoming sexually mature and most girls have already entered puberty.

Along with their intense connection to peers, fourteens may also be strongly devoted and loyal to a sport or a musical instrument, to body piercing, or to a friendship or an idol. They're practicing fidelity, which helps prepare them to participate as disciplined, loving partners and full-fledged citizens when they become adults. Traditions, guidelines, customs, and passage experiences that recognize fourteens' dawning adulthood help them further reflect on and practice fidelity: think family "passage parties," the first solo hike, new responsibilities at home, or privileges at school reserved for students in their fourteenth year.

Although experiences that help fourteens develop fidelity may be offered by family, heritage, or the larger culture, school is the main structured social setting where students encounter and learn to meet society's demands. How a school is structured, the way it places demands on students, and how it supports their growth are critically important factors in the development of healthy young adults.

Whether at home or at school, the process of identifying themselves as separate, almost-adult individuals means that fourteens want to do everything their way, to have freedom, to be on their own. They may not always be good at following directions, but they're great at inventing new ones. These students constantly look for opportunities to decide for themselves what they will do—get a part-time job, join a rock band, or play a sport. Challenging adult authority becomes an almost visceral reaction, one that may be accompanied by eye-rolling, hair-tossing, and other scornful expressions that serve as distancing gestures.

For all their outward bravado and sense of sureness, though, fourteens are easily embarrassed by activities that may cause them to appear uncool in the eyes of their peers. Such activities may include working hard in school, dressing up, or going out to eat with parents. In fact, parents—being seen with them, or having them wear unacceptable clothes, drive an old car, or say the wrong thing—are often acute sources of distress for fourteens as they strive to separate from the adults closest to them.

Yet, as much as fourteens push parents and other adults away, they crave strong connections with them and want and expect adults to keep them safe. Truly listening to fourteens—acknowledging their presence, confirming their experience, respecting

14-Year-Olds at Home

- ◆ Push adults away as they strive for independence; at the same time, they need to know adults will keep them safe

- ◆ Are often embarrassed to be seen with their parents, and are fiercely critical of parents' dress, habits, friends, and ideas; patience, humor, a listening ear, and willingness to consider their requests and set limits as needed will help negotiations during this tumultuous time

- ◆ Value peer connections above almost anything else; often want to go to school when they don't feel well just so they can connect with friends

them, and enjoying them—is one powerful way to connect. Parents can set aside a regular, structured time for family listening and discussion—and hold to it despite their teenager's protestations. Schools can provide counseling, peer tutoring, advisories, and opportunities for community service.

Negotiating helps, too. Without giving in to every demand (or to arguing, tears, and fervent pleading), parents and teachers can thoughtfully consider fourteens' input and adjust homework, curfews, chores, and afterschool activities in small but meaningful ways, increasing their freedom and accountability while still holding them to high standards. Each negotiation offers a chance to practice adult-level responsibility—and who better to practice with than the people who care about them the most?

Being fourteen is hard work—for the teens themselves as well as the parents and teachers who guide them. Adult restraint and patience help enormously, as does reminding ourselves to weigh the sometimes exasperating behavior of fourteens against the wonder of an adult personality emerging before our eyes.

Typical Growth Patterns of 14-Year-Olds

PHYSICAL DEVELOPMENT

◆ Very energetic; need as much physical release as possible through brief periods of physical activity outdoors or a stretch/brain break in the classroom

◆ If given time to reenergize, often perform and behave better in the afternoon

◆ Need lots of exercise, snacks, and sleep

◆ Girls are almost fully developed

◆ Growth spurts continue for boys, and their upper body strength begins to develop

◆ Both boys and girls are more interested in sex; some are sexually active

SOCIAL AND EMOTIONAL DEVELOPMENT

◆ Learn well in small discussion or cooperative learning groups; benefit from working with a wide variety of groupmates in their different classes

◆ Enjoy talking about current events, both formally in class and informally with peers

CONTINUED ▶

◆ Often say "I'm bored" to mean "I don't understand," or say that work is too easy when they find it plenty challenging; this is "face-saving" behavior typical of this age

◆ Typically loud and rambunctious; balance in classroom expectations is important (that is, requiring silence sometimes, but not always)

◆ Are in a "know-it-all" stage, in which they especially dislike and respond poorly to adult lectures, feeling they know what will be said once they hear the first few words

◆ Faces and body language often express "contempt," a way of distancing themselves from teachers and parents as they move toward more adult independence

◆ Enjoy engaging in group discussion and tackling big ideas

◆ Complain about homework, but often enjoy the challenge if not overwhelmed; middle school teachers benefit from coordinating and limiting homework to essential and interesting assignments used immediately in class the next day

COGNITIVE CAPACITY

◆ Respond well to academic variety and challenge, especially if given opportunities to propose and help plan and organize the challenges

◆ Enjoy and do well with lengthier projects if assignments are "chunked" with clear timelines

- Intrigued by research and putting together research reports in the proper format; sometimes, interest in form takes precedence over depth of content

- Many show increased interest in math and science; like to explore the unknown in science

- Better at figuring out cause and effect and doing abstract thinking and testing of hypotheses

- Like learning how things work; thrive on field trips to factories and science museums

ETHICS AND SELF-DIRECTION

- More willing to admit an error and try something a second or third time

- Very aware of problems in the larger world and invested in learning more and finding solutions

- Peer pressure may lead them to feel that excelling in school is uncool

- Exploratory classes, service projects, sports, and other group undertakings often lead to a first career interest

- May develop distinctive sense of humor; can be extremely funny and creative

◆ Crave adult connections even while fighting for their own identity; need adults to listen and negotiate rules and requirements, but set clear boundaries and deadlines

◆ Adult personality continues to mature

◆ Take pleasure in developing individual skills (for example, music, art, or crafts) that express their emerging adult intelligence

◆ Like having a chance to evaluate and improve their own work and can also constructively critique other students' work

◆ Interested in learning and discovery as a means of answering the "Who am I?" question

◆ Like to cram as much into each day as they possibly can; stay up late and have trouble getting up early

How Growth Patterns Relate to Learning

READING

Provide opportunities for students this age to:

◆ Use literary themes to support their quest for identity; especially affected by coming-of-age novels from different historical periods

◆ Sample many genres, such as song lyrics, poetry, drama, short stories, and novels

◆ Study how literary elements interweave—for example, how characterization can advance the plot of a story

◆ Express their understanding of the difference between fact and opinion

◆ Use textual references in writing and discussion

◆ Use language as a tool for different purposes (for example, to tell a story versus advertise a product); enjoy presenting in class more than at younger ages

◆ Participate in class read-alouds, which they continue to find an appealing springboard for discussion

◆ Explore meanings of words and develop a broader vocabulary

WRITING

Expect from these students:

- **Writing** Interest in choosing appropriate genre (poem, play, story) in which to represent their ideas; experimentation with different voices, often tied in with literature they're studying; writing from different points of view; more deliberate use of grammatical constructions for stylistic reasons; beginning use of conventional footnotes, endnotes, and bibliographic entries

- **Spelling** Functional for most; use of spell checkers is helpful when writing on computers

- **Writing themes** Motivation to write in preparation for activities such as debates and mock trials, which increasingly require them to structure and defend their thinking; use of literary themes as a springboard for writing assignments and creative writing; ability to do longer research papers related to thematic studies; willingness to write journals with adults (teens and adults respond to each other's entries) as a means of sorting out issues in their own lives and the larger world; willingness to create posters for school plays or write articles for the school paper

---

MATH

Provide opportunities for students this age to:

- Review all operations, with special emphasis on ratio and proportion; present different ways to approach and solve a problem or "question of the day"

- Read and use graphs, particularly circle and bar graphs, to make a point or summarize an argument

- Explore number systems with numbers other than 10 as their base

- Work with the binary number system

- Solve algebraic and word problems with one or more unknowns

- Study formal algebra

ACROSS THE CURRICULUM
(including social studies, languages, science, special areas)

Provide opportunities for students this age to:

- Move around and take regular stretch breaks

- Take on academic challenges and propose projects

- Participate in cooperative learning groups in a variety of subjects; take part in structured discussions about big ideas

- Explore concepts in science; engage in proposing and testing hypotheses

- Begin to explore potential career interests through classes, projects, and after-school activities

- Engage in constructive criticism of each other's work as well as self-evaluation

APPENDIX A

Resources for Educators

CHILD DEVELOPMENT

Ames, Louise Bates. *Arnold Gesell: Themes of His Work*. New York: Human Sciences Press, 1989.

Bodrova, Elena, and Deborah J. Leong. *Tools of the Mind: The Vygotskian Approach to Early Childhood Education*. 2nd ed. Upper Saddle River, NJ: Pearson/Merrill Prentice Hall, 2007.

Cohen, Dorothy H. *The Learning Child: Guidelines for Parents and Teachers*. New York: Pantheon Books, 1972.

Crain, William. *Theories of Development: Concepts and Applications*. 6th ed. Boston: Prentice Hall, 2011.

Erikson, Erik. *Identity: Youth and Crisis*. New York: W. W. Norton & Company, 1968.

Ilg, Frances L., Louise Bates Ames, and Sidney M. Baker. *Child Behavior: The Classic Child Care Manual from the Gesell Institute of Human Development*. Rev. ed. New York: William Morrow Paperbacks, 1992.

Montessori, Maria. *The Montessori Method*. Trans. A. E. George. Reprint. New York: Barnes & Noble Publishing, 1912/2003.

Piaget, Jean. *The Language and Thought of the Child*. Trans. Marjorie and Ruth Gabain. Abingdon, UK: Routledge and Kegan Paul, 1926/1959.

————. *The Moral Judgment of the Child.* Trans. Marjorie Gabain. Foreword by William Damon. New York: Free Press Paperbacks, 1932/1997.

Pianta, Robert, ed. *Handbook of Early Childhood Education.* New York: Guilford Press, 2012.

Pratt, Caroline. *I Learn from Children: An Adventure in Progressive Education.* Reprint ed. Introduction by Ian Frazier. New York: Grove Press, 2014.

Steiner, Rudolf. *An Introduction to Waldorf Education and Other Essays.* Redford, VA: Wilder Publications, 2008.

Vygotsky, Lev. *Thought and Language.* Revised ed. Trans. A. Kozulin. Boston: MIT Press, 1934/1986.

CULTURE AND DEVELOPMENT

Ashton-Warner, Sylvia. *Teacher.* Foreword by Maxine Hong Kingston. New York: Simon & Schuster, 1986.

Brisk, Maria Estela, and Margaret M. Harrington. *Literacy and Bilingualism: A Handbook for ALL Teachers.* 2nd ed. New York: Routledge, 2015.

Comer, James P., and Alvin F. Poussaint. *Raising Black Children: Two Leading Psychiatrists Confront the Educational, Social and Emotional Problems Facing Black Children.* New York: Plume, 1992.

Kessler, Rachael. *The Soul of Education: Helping Students Find Connection, Compassion, and Character at School.* Alexandria, VA: Association for Supervision and Curriculum Development, 2000.

Lightfoot, Cynthia, Michael Cole, and Sheila R. Cole. *The Development of Children.* 7th ed. New York: Worth, 2012.

Nieto, Sonia. *The Light in Their Eyes: Creating Multicultural Learning Communities*. 10th anniversary ed. New York: Teachers College Press, 2009.

Rogoff, Barbara. *Apprenticeship in Thinking: Cognitive Development in Social Context*. New York: Oxford University Press, 1990.

———. *The Cultural Nature of Human Development*. New York: Oxford University Press, 2003.

Tatum, Beverly Daniel. *"Why Are All the Black Kids Sitting Together in the Cafeteria?" And Other Conversations About Race*. Revised ed. New York: Basic Books, 2017.

Tomlinson, Carol Ann. *How to Differentiate Instruction in Academically Diverse Classrooms*. 3rd ed. Alexandria, VA: Association for Supervision and Curriculum Development, 2017.

Vilson, José. *This Is Not a Test: A New Narrative on Race, Class, and Education*. Chicago: Haymarket Books, 2014.

NEUROSCIENCE AND DEVELOPMENT

Cozolino, Louis. *The Social Neuroscience of Education: Optimizing Attachment and Learning in the Classroom*. New York: W. W. Norton, 2013.

Davidson, Richard J. *The Emotional Life of Your Brain: How Its Unique Patterns Affect the Way You Think, Feel, and Live—and How You Can Change Them*. With Sharon Begley. New York: Hudson Street Press, 2012.

Duckworth, Angela. *Grit: The Power of Passion and Perseverance*. New York: Scribner, 2016.

Goleman, Daniel. *Destructive Emotions, and How We Can Overcome Them*. New York: Bantam Books, 2003.

Hammond, Zaretta. *Culturally Responsive Teaching and the Brain: Promoting Authentic Engagement and Rigor Among Culturally and Linguistically Diverse Students.* Thousand Oaks, CA: Corwin, 2015.

Jennings, Patricia A. *Mindfulness for Teachers: Simple Skills for Peace and Productivity in the Classroom.* New York: W. W. Norton, 2015.

Jensen, Eric. *Teaching with the Brain in Mind.* 2nd ed. Alexandria, VA: Association for Supervision and Curriculum Development, 2005.

Lieberman, Matthew D. *Social: Why Our Brains Are Wired to Connect.* New York: Broadway Books, 2013.

Siegel, Daniel J. *The Mindful Brain: Reflection and Attunement in the Cultivation of Well-Being.* New York: W. W. Norton, 2007.

———. *Pocket Guide to Interpersonal Neurobiology: An Integrative Handbook of the Mind.* New York: W. W. Norton, 2012.

Stern, Daniel N. *The Present Moment in Psychotherapy and Everyday Life.* New York: W. W. Norton, 2004.

Sylwester, Robert. *A Biological Brain in a Cultural Classroom: Enhancing Cognitive and Social Development Through Collaborative Classroom Management.* 2nd ed. Thousand Oaks, CA: Corwin, 2003.

Resources for Parents

Carlsson-Paige, Nancy. *Taking Back Childhood: A Proven Road Map for Raising Confident, Creative, Compassionate Kids.* New York: Plume, 2009.

Crain, William. *Reclaiming Childhood: Letting Children Be Children in Our Achievement-Oriented Society.* New York: Henry Holt, 2003.

Elkind, David. *The Power of Play: Learning What Comes Naturally.* Boston: Da Capo Press, 2007.

Faber, Adele, and Elaine Mazlish. *How to Talk So Kids Will Listen and Listen So Kids Will Talk.* New York: Scribner, 2012.

Fox, Jenifer. *Your Child's Strengths: A Guide for Parents and Teachers.* New York: Penguin, 2008.

Galinsky, Ellen. *Mind in the Making: The Seven Essential Life Skills Every Child Needs.* New York: HarperCollins, 2010.

Hirsh-Pasek, Kathy, and Roberta Michnick Golinkoff. *Einstein Never Used Flash Cards: How Our Children Really Learn—And Why They Need to Play More and Memorize Less.* With Diane Eyer. New York: MJF Books, 2003.

Hunter, Latoya. *The Diary of Latoya Hunter: My First Year in Junior High.* New York: Vintage, 1993.

Lawrence-Lightfoot, Sara. *Growing Each Other Up: When Our Children Become Our Teachers.* Chicago: University of Chicago Press, 2016.

———. *Respect: An Exploration.* New York: Basic Books, 2000.

Louv, Richard. *Last Child in the Woods: Saving Our Children from Nature-Deficit Disorder.* Revised and expanded ed. Chapel Hill, NC: Algonquin Books, 2005.

McAdoo, Harriette Pipes, ed. *Black Families.* 4th ed. Thousand Oaks, CA: Sage Publications, 2007.

Miller, Karen. *Ages and Stages: Developmental Descriptions and Activities, Birth through Eight Years.* Revised ed. West Palm Beach, FL: Telshare Publishing, 2001

Nelsen, Jane. *Positive Discipline: The Classic Guide to Helping Children Develop Self-Discipline, Responsibility, Cooperation, and Problem-Solving Skills.* Revised and updated ed. New York: Ballantine Books, 2006.

Payne, Kim John. *Simplicity Parenting: Using the Extraordinary Power of Less to Raise Calmer, Happier, and More Secure Kids.* With Lisa M. Ross. New York: Ballantine Books, 2009.

Staley, Betty. *Between Form and Freedom: A Practical Guide to the Teenage Years.* 2nd ed. Stroud, UK: Hawthorn Press, 2009.

Wolf, Anthony E. *Get Out of My Life, but First Could You Drive Me and Cheryl to the Mall? A Parent's Guide to the New Teenager.* New York: Farrar, Straus and Giroux, 2002.

———. *I'd Listen to My Parents if They'd Just Shut Up: What to Say and Not Say When Parenting Teens.* New York: HarperCollins, 2011.

———. *The Secret of Parenting: How to Be in Charge of Today's Kids—from Toddlers to Preteens—Without Threats or Punishment.* New York: Farrar, Straus and Giroux, 2000.

The Birthday Cluster Exercise

Yardsticks contains lots of useful information about what children need at any given age in school. Yet a first question many teachers will have is, "How do I apply this to a whole class of children? There is such a range of development in any class and every year my classes are so different."

The most practical way I know to apply the general developmental characteristics in the book is to use the birthday cluster exercise. Here's how to do it.

| Create a Chronological Listing

Although chronological age does not necessarily correlate directly to developmental age, you can use students' chronological ages to get a sense of the overall developmental abilities and behaviors you're likely to see in a class.

A simple way to do this is to list the students in the class from youngest to oldest, using a "year, month" format to show each child's age (for example, 9 years, 2 months). From a complete list of children's ages (see page 184) you can easily see the range of chronological ages you'll be teaching.

See Where the Birthdays Cluster

Once you've created your chronological list, you need to see where most birthdays cluster as of a given date—say on September 1. In our sample fourth grade chart, the greatest number of children are at 9 years, 7 months, on September 1 (five out of twenty-two), with another four at 9 years, 9 months. So the birthday cluster in this classroom is in the 9 years, 7 to 9 months range. Creating a bar graph (as shown on page 185) can help you see the cluster.

Use What You've Learned

When you've completed this exercise, you'll know whether the children you'll be teaching form a class that is, overall, young, old, or somewhere in between. In our sample fourth grade class, the cluster in the 9 years, 7 to 9 month range, plus the many children who are ten plus or minus a month, make it, overall, an old class.

What do you do now?

- ◆ Plan for a fourth grade class beginning the year with mostly older nine-year-old and ten-year-old developmental characteristics. Look back through the book at the classroom implications for these ages. Think about your room arrangement and about the curriculum activities that will most engage this class as a whole.

◆ Think about how the class will be different in the second half of the year, when many children (more than half by March) will most likely be exhibiting ten-year-old developmental characteristics, with one or two possibly exhibiting eleven-year-old characteristics. You'll need to adjust approaches to classroom organization, instruction, classroom responsibilities, homework, and many other areas to accommodate students' shifting developmental needs.

◆ Consider the potential needs and problem areas of the children on the younger and older ends of the spectrum and think about how you will address those needs as you see how the students respond to daily classroom life.

Sample fourth grade chronological age chart, 2017–2018 school year

Name	Date of Birth	Chronological Age	
		9/1/17	**3/1/18**
Fernando	7/31/08	9 years, 1 month	9 years, 7 months
Austin	6/25/08	9 years, 2 months	9 years, 8 months
Justine	6/21/08	9 years, 2 months	9 years, 8 months
Shawana	6/12/08	9 years, 2 months	9 years, 8 months
Carolynne	2/6/08	9 years, 6 months	10 years, 0 months
Emma	1/14/08	9 years, 7 months	10 years, 1 month
Helena	1/27/08	9 years, 7 months	10 years, 1 month
Amario	1/26/08	9 years, 7 months	10 years, 1 month
Ginger	1/7/08	9 years, 7 months	10 years, 1 month
Martin	1/4/08	9 years, 7 months	10 years, 1 month
Ashleigh	11/30/07	9 years, 9 months	10 years, 3 months
Ben	11/29/07	9 years, 9 months	10 years, 3 months
Linda	11/18/07	9 years, 9 months	10 years, 3 months
Clemmie	11/4/07	9 years, 9 months	10 years, 3 months
Mack	10/18/07	9 years, 10 months	10 years, 4 months
Gawain	9/19/07	9 years, 11 months	10 years, 5 months

Name	Date of Birth	Chronological Age	
		9/1/17	**3/1/18**
Lupe	9/13/07	9 years, 11 months	10 years, 5 months
Bonnie	9/3/07	9 years, 11 months	10 years, 5 months
Liam	8/9/07	10 years, 0 months	10 years, 6 months
Heath	8/9/07	10 years, 0 months	10 years, 6 months
Nadia	8/2/07	10 years, 0 months	10 years, 6 months
Dan	7/25/07	10 years, 1 month	10 years, 7 months

NOTE: Classes are sometimes older or younger than average, depending on kindergarten cut-off dates and other factors. The students in this class, for example, are older than average.

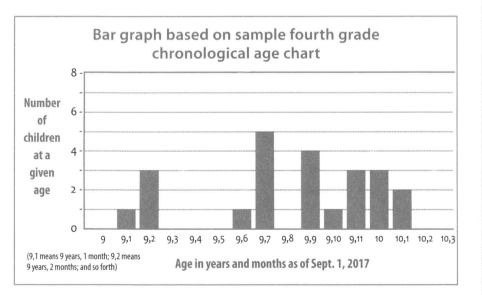

(9,1 means 9 years, 1 month; 9,2 means 9 years, 2 months; and so forth)

ACKNOWLEDGMENTS

✳

This book would never have been written without my close association with Jackie Haines and many other wonderful professionals at Gesell Institute of Child Development, where I was first trained in developmental observation and later became a certified trainer.

Marlynn K. Clayton and Deborah Porter taught my children and taught with me in two schools during our careers. We learned much together, and I remain grateful for all they did to support me as a young principal and parent many years ago.

Thanks to other colleagues at Northeast Foundation for Children (now known as Center for Responsive Schools) and Greenfield Center School: particularly, co-founders Ruth Sidney Charney and Jay Lord. Thanks also to Roxann Kriete, Mary Beth Forton, and others who created a publishing house that has helped broaden the reach of *Responsive Classroom* for 30-plus years.

I am grateful to teachers, parents, and students, too numerous to name, whom I've had the privilege to teach and learn from over the past forty-five years. I feel compelled, however, to name and acknowledge a special few: Linda and Elizabeth Crawford, Jo Devlin, Jon and Faith Ball, and Eve Eisman, for journeying with me on the educational frontier. Likewise, my colleagues in the Courage to Teach movement with whom I have kept company in reflective listening and learning for the last twenty years, especially Pamela Seigle, Lisa Sankowski, Rick and Marcy Jackson, Terry Chadsey, and Parker J. Palmer.

Special thanks to Lynn Bechtel, CRS managing editor, and CRS senior editor Elizabeth Nash for their graciousness, patience, and helpfulness in the process of preparing this revision; and to the current director of publications, Christine Freitas, for her oversight.

Finally, thanks to Heather, Jon, Son, Isaiah, Lily, Belle, extended family, and close friends, for all the support I have received from each and every one of you when I needed it the most. And, of course, without the love and companionship Reenie shared with me for over fifty years, this book would never have continued appearing.

Robert (Chip) Wood
Buckland, MA
December 2017

ABOUT THE AUTHOR

✳

 For forty-five years, Robert (Chip) Wood has worked on behalf of children from preschool through eighth grade as a classroom teacher, teaching principal, and teacher educator. After studying at the Gesell Institute of Human Development early in his career, Chip made developmentally based teaching the center of his educational practice. His core belief: knowing what children at each age are developmentally capable of doing physically, socially, emotionally, and cognitively enables respectful, successful teaching of all children—no matter their life circumstances or cultural background. A co-developer of *Responsive Classroom* and co-founder of Northeast Foundation for Children (now Center for Responsive Schools), Chip has served as principal of two public schools and was co-founder of Greenfield Center School. He is a facilitator for the Center for Courage & Renewal and co-creator of Leading Together, an approach focused on strengthening the adult community of schools.

ABOUT THE PUBLISHER

✳

Center for Responsive Schools, Inc., a not-for-profit educational organization, is the developer of *Responsive Classroom*®, an evidence-based education approach associated with greater teacher effectiveness, higher student achievement, and improved school climate. *Responsive Classroom* practices help educators build competencies in four interrelated domains: engaging academics, positive community, effective management, and developmentally responsive teaching. We offer the following resources for educators:

PROFESSIONAL DEVELOPMENT SERVICES

- Workshops for K–8 educators (locations around the country and internationally)
- On-site consulting services to support implementation
- Resources for site-based study
- Annual conferences for K–8 educators

PUBLICATIONS AND RESOURCES

- Books on a wide variety of *Responsive Classroom* topics
- Free monthly newsletter
- Extensive library of free articles on our website

For details, contact:

Responsive Classroom®

Center for Responsive Schools, Inc.
85 Avenue A, P.O. Box 718
Turners Falls, Massachusetts 01376-0718

800-360-6332 ◆ www.responsiveclassroom.org
info@responsiveclassroom.org